LEADING *from* YOUR STRENGTHS

2

BUILDING INTIMACY IN YOUR SMALL GROUP

JOHN TRENT

RODNEY COX ERIC TOOKER

BROADMAN
&HOLMAN
PUBLISHERS

NASHVILLE, TENNESSEE

Dedication

This book is dedicated to every shall group leader who is passionate about helping the members of their small group grow closer together and strengthen their relationships in the pursuit of intimacy.

0-8054-3066-0

Published by Broadman & Holman Publishers,
Nashville, Tennessee

Published in assoociation with Alive Communications, Inc., 7660 Goddard Street, Suite 200, Colorado Springs, CO 80970

Dewey Decimel Classification: 302.3
Subject Heading: SMALL GROUPS \ COMMUNICATION IN SMALL GROUPS \ GROUP PROBLEM SOLVING

Leading From Your Strengths™ is a registered trademark of Insights International, Inc. in Scottsdale, Arizona.

Unless otherwise stated, all Scripture is taken from the NASB, the New American Standard Bible, © the Lockman Foundation, 1960, 1962, 1963, 1968, 1971, 1972, 1973, 1975, 1977, 1995. Used by permission.

All names and locations used in the stories found in this book have been changed to protect the actual person's true identity.

1 2 3 4 5 6 7 8 10 09 08 07 06 05

Contents

Acknowledgments

The authors would like to acknowledge and express our gratitude for the wonderful small-group ministries of our home churches, Covenant Community Church and Scottsdale Bible Church, in Scottsdale, Arizona.

The authors would also like to acknowledge the invaluable contribution of Dave and Dawn Lind of Focus on Purpose (www.FocusonPurpose.com) in creating the small-group study found in Part III of this book. Their contribution will help small groups everywhere begin their journey toward achieving intimacy.

Part I

Making a Powerful Difference in Your Small Group

Introduction
Reaching the Summit for Your Small Group

THANK YOU FOR picking up this book!

The fact that you picked this book off the shelf is a clear reflection of your desire to see your small group become even closer, more encouraging, and a more God-honoring place than ever before! You're joining thousands of people across our country finding strength, healing, hope, and God's wisdom in small numbers. By committing yourself to a small band of brothers and sisters, equally serious about their faith and genuine friendships, you can absolutely see lives transformed, hurts healed, and a God-honoring future become more real than ever before.

Those are some of the benefits of being in a small group. But we realize that there is risk in being part of a small group as well.

In part, that's why we picked the metaphor of a mountain climbing expedition that flows throughout this book. Not that we're saying closeness and caring in your small group is as hard to reach as scaling Mount Everest, but you can learn *many lessons* from expert climbing teams.

While you may not be aware of it, every expedition stops at four camps on their way to the summit of Mount Everest. After Base Camp (a mere seventeen thousand feet above sea level), climbers make four stops on their way to the world's greatest view.

With your small group we'll be urging you to follow that same approach. At Base Camp you will see how crucial it is to gather the

3

right equipment and, most of all, to get to know those in your small group as well and as quickly as possible. For your small group, Base Camp will include the strong encouragement to take a powerful online assessment that can help you discover your own God-given strengths and those of each person in your small group. Just by going online and taking the Leading From Your Strengths™ assessment, we truly believe you can get to know those on your "climbing team" better than after months of casual conversation.

After Base Camp, the four stopping points for climbers are called C1, C2, C3, and C4. You'll find there are four stopping points on the way to intimacy for your small group as well.

And here's a crucial thing to understand: To make a successful Mount Everest climb, you can't skip a stopping point. In fact, time at each level helps you acclimate to the climb. Also, in a Mount Everest expedition, they actually go back down a level or two, then climb back up to a higher stopping point. That's purposeful! Going back down for a short time isn't a failure but a time to gather strength to go even higher!

Can you see how this concept applies to your small group? With any real small group, there will be weeks when it seems like you've made it to C3 only to find the next week you're back down to C2. That's fine! Times of struggle can be just as valuable as times of excitement and growth.

With your small group you'll stop at Base Camp to take time to pick up needed equipment and get to know your climbing mates. Then you'll be encouraged to work your way toward four camps on your way to becoming a world-class small group. Instead of these camps being called C1, C2, C3, and C4, we've put names to them:

- Commitment—the starting point for all small groups that will get you through the trials and joys that follow.
- Honesty—to share who you really are—warts, imperfections, and all.
- Acceptance—to become the kind of safe place where unconditional love for others allows you to open up and share strengths and imperfections.
- Trust—the maturing fruit that comes from building up commitment, honesty, and acceptance over time.

These are the four camps or goal points you'll find highlighted in the chapters that follow. Just reaching any one of them is worthy of praise for your small group. But after the first four camps, you're ready for the summit. For at the top you'll find:

- Intimacy—that closeness that comes from being the kind of lifelong, committed, caring brothers and sisters in Christ that we all long for this side of heaven.

In the pages that follow, you'll learn a great deal about supporting one another, understanding one another's strengths, and coming to the aid of each person in your small group. By doing this, you can reach heights you might have never thought possible, and that's whether you live at the base of Mount Rainier, on the plains of Kansas, or on the shores of North Carolina.

So once again, thanks for your commitment to taking one step at a time toward the best small-group experience you've ever had. Let us know how we can help you, and if you will, share with us your small group success story as well by e-mailing us at feedback@leadingfromyourstrengths.com. If you'll give us written permission, we'd love to share your story with others on our Web site, as you move higher and higher in loving the Lord and one another in your small group.

May the Lord bless, encourage, and strengthen you and each member of your small group!

John Trent, Ph.D.   Rodney Cox   Eric Tooker
The Leading From Your Strengths™ Team

Chapter One
Trouble in Small-Group Paradise

"I'VE NEVER BEEN in a small group that worked."

Jeff hoped his reply would cut off any further debate about whether he would be joining Mark's small group meeting that night. Jeff was one of Mark's closest friends at the church, but that didn't stop Jeff from resisting every effort Mark made to include Jeff and his wife Liz in the home fellowship group that Mark led every Friday night. Mark had heard all of Jeff's excuses before.

"It takes too long to get to know everyone. Once you do, there is always conflict over who will take care of the kids, how much to pay the babysitter, how long to meet, and what to study. It's more hassle than it's worth."

Jeff knew that small groups were supposed to build unity among an otherwise diverse group of believers, but to him they were more likely to spark controversy than closeness. Mark had a hard time empathizing with Jeff because all of his experiences in small groups had been positive.

"Jeff, a small group is really the best way to get connected on a deeper level with other people from church. God wants us to be in deep, personal relationships with other people. He never meant for us to walk alone. Linda and I are able to build up and encourage other believers, and we always get back more than we give!"

Mark's plea fell on deaf ears. Jeff had tried small groups, and, for him, they had failed. He was simply not willing to make the effort

again. Mark had been turned down before when he invited people
to become part of his small group.

*What made this particular rejection more frustrating and surpris-
ing than others was that Jeff was the senior pastor of his church!*

For most small-group leaders, the situation that Mark found
himself in is far too common. He is a committed, effective small-
group leader in a church where the senior pastor is not a part of the
small-group ministry. Sometimes a pastor may not actively oppose
small groups; in fact, he may even support them, but only theoreti-
cally. Most small-group experts agree that if the senior pastor is not
actively promoting small groups or an active participant in them, it
is much more difficult for a small-group ministry to prosper.

If your senior pastor is fully on board with your developing a
close-knit small group, that's a great starting point. Yet even in the
worst-case scenario above, people like Mark can build their small
group into the kind of authentic biblical community where intimacy
and genuine caring for one another becomes the hallmark of the
group. In fact, it can even become the kind of place that draws
someone like Jeff in once he sees the changed lives and deepened
commitments a small group can foster.

BIBLICAL STRENGTH TRAINING
THROUGH SMALL GROUPS

IT'S A SMALL-GROUP WORLD

In most churches today it is a small-group world. Small groups
are quickly becoming an integral part of most people's journey of
faith. There are churches *with* small groups, churches *of* small
groups, and churches that *are* small groups. There are churches that
are in transition from one to an other. What is rare these days is a
church without small groups. Small groups have gone in and out of
fashion for decades, but most would admit that the small-group
ministry movement that has grown and flourished in the last several years is different and lasting. Small-group ministry is rooted in
the church's past, but it is viewed by most now as the future of the
church as well.

Revival is breaking out in the local church, and it is happening
through small groups. The small-group movement today is building
up the local church by empowering the average person in the pew

to affect the lives of other people in the church. Romans 12 gives us encouragement to do just that. God composed the body of Christ by giving each person unique strengths and gifts that are to be used in service to one another for the common good. Small groups, because they consist of life-on-life interactions, supply the perfect vehicle to do just that.

A small group is not an end in itself; rather, it is a means to an end. The popularity of small groups is driven by their increasing influence and effectiveness in transforming lives. Small groups can turn lost, lonely, isolated individuals into people who are able to get beyond the hurt of past broken relationships and enter into new relationships based on trust, honesty, acceptance, and love. Small groups are now an option for an increasing number of churches that are finding them the only effective way for caring, nurturing, loving, and serving the body in the local church.

The rationale for having a small-group ministry is obviously compelling, not to mention biblical. Acts 20:20 describes how the apostle Paul grew the early church by teaching believers "publicly and from house to house." This verse illustrates the common church strategy of emphasizing the Sunday worship time coupled with small-group gatherings during the week. In doing so, Paul was building on the example Jesus set. Jesus called a small group of men to walk with him in his earthly ministry, and they lived in community. Jesus chose to share his life with twelve men and, through them, to touch the masses.

But for all the benefits of being in a small group, they're not easy! In fact, many people have had anything but a positive experience and wonder whether small groups are worth the investment of time and energy at all!

ARE SMALL GROUPS WORTH THE HASSLE?

At its worst a small group is a collection of diverse, needy, isolated people who come together for regular meetings; and that's it. No community is developed. No unity is fostered. And no intimacy is achieved. At its best a small group can take this same collection of diverse, needy, isolated people and, through the power of the Holy Spirit, knit them together into an authentic community marked by a deep intimacy. The kind of intimacy where masks come off and people are unconditionally loved for who they really are. The kind of intimacy that is evidenced by sacrificial caring for one another. The kind of intimacy that Jesus begged God to give his disciples in his high priestly prayer. "I do not ask on behalf of these alone, but for those also who believe in Me through their word; *that they may all be one*; even as You, Father, are in Me and I in You, that they also may be in Us, so that the world may believe that You sent Me" (John 17:20–21, emphasis added). Jesus wanted the disciples to experience the same kind of intimacy with one another that he experiences with the Father and the Holy Spirit. He wants the same for each one of us today. And one of the best places to experience that intimacy is in a small group.

Intimate means "belonging to or characterizing one's deepest nature." While it's not practical to believe you will have a deep, intimate relationship with everyone in your small group, intimacy with others in your group should be a goal. Make closer relationships in your small group a matter of prayer, and find ways to connect relationally to others in the group. This helps the group develop a network of meaningful relationships that transforms the group into a loving, exciting fellowship of believers.

If your small-group experience is not like the one we have described, there is probably good reason. Many obstacles need to be overcome to build intimacy. Because we are sinful people, anytime there is a group where relationships intersect, there is the potential for mistrust, conflict, miscommunication, and disharmony. Obstacles like these confront every small group. Removing these obstacles, or better yet, avoiding them in the first place, is the key to clearing the way for intimacy. Steering clear of or removing obstacles like these in a small-group setting is a daunting task but one that must be undertaken for any small group to become what God desires and what each small group member truly needs.

Are small groups worth the hassle? The apostle Paul answers a resounding yes!

The early church was comprised of nothing but small home-fellowship groups. They met in large groups for corporate worship, but the day-to-day fellowship happened in small community groups meeting in the homes of members. Paul underscored the importance of this fellowship by saying, "For just as we have many members in one body and all the members do not have the same function, *so we, who are many, are one body in Christ, and individually members one of another*" (Rom. 12:4–5, emphasis added). We are united through our collective faith in Christ, a unified body of diverse believers, no longer an assortment of isolated individuals.

TO GOD BE THE GLORY!

Why did God create us with a need for relationships? Why should I work to develop relationships despite the difficulty, pain, and heartache they can cause? Why should I labor to create intimacy among the relationships in my small group? The answer to each of these questions is the same. *For his glory.* The apostle Paul wrote, "Now may the God who gives perseverance and encouragement grant you to be of the same mind with one another according to Christ Jesus, *so that with one accord you may with one voice glorify the God and Father of our Lord Jesus Christ*" (Rom. 15:5–6, emphasis added). John Piper once said:

A group of people learning how to love each other in the power of the Gospel and in the power of the Spirit glorifies God more than single individuals relating to Christ in isolation. That's not hard to understand. It's easier to stay at home and watch TV than to get together with people different from you and carry their burdens in prayer and minister to them with your gifts and strategize with them to reach the lost. But God doesn't get more glory when you just do the easy thing. He gets more glory when you depend on him to help you do the hard thing— and especially when you do it with the joy of hope.[1]

The church exists to glorify God, and the glory he receives is magnified when we determine to come together and intentionally pursue relationships for the express purpose of loving one another as Christ loved us. It is no small task to undertake, but it is no small gift to give back to God when we love one another for his glory alone.

How do we do it? We do it by understanding the unique strengths that God has blessed each one of us with and using them in loving and serving one another. These strengths are a gift from God, not something we deserve or earn. When we put them to use, we will surely fail unless we do it through God's power rather than our own effort. The strengths themselves, as well as the ability to use them, are by God's grace. Because we cannot boast, God gets the glory that is rightfully his. "Whoever speaks, is to do so as one who is speaking the utterances of God; whoever serves is to do so as one who is serving by the strength which God supplies; so that in all things God may be glorified through Jesus Christ, to whom belongs the glory and dominion forever and ever. Amen" (1 Pet. 4:11).

Our faith in Christ unites us to him. That same faith unites us to one another. Our responsibility before God is to stand ready to do the work he has for us. That necessarily includes finding out what our God-given strengths are, embracing those strengths, developing those strengths and using them, through the power he supplies, to minister to our brothers and sisters in Christ. This does not all have to happen in small groups, but there are few vehicles better suited to empower us to accomplish this task. After all, a small group is a foretaste of what we will experience in heaven. There we will be engaged in active service to our Lord with one another. There we will live in eternal fellowship with the same brothers and sisters whom we unite with today!

Whatever kind of small group you are in or whatever kind of small group you are considering joining, you can be faithful to this calling. Your group can develop the kind of intimacy we have been describing. Your small group can become a place where members share, trust, and walk through life together. The purpose of this book is to teach you the principles that will enable you to do just that.

In the next several chapters, we're going to use a mountain-climbing analogy that will run throughout the book. We'll talk about Base Camp and the four stopping points, each one preparing us to go higher and reach the top. While we could go on and on about the biblical basis and the practical benefits of small groups, we'll be leaving any more discussion of benefits for other books. What we want to do in this book is help you find the right path up to the summit of intimacy.

In a mountain-climbing expedition, picking the right path up to the top is crucial to the whole group succeeding or failing in their efforts. We want you to succeed, to pick safe paths, and to avoid dangerous pitfalls. This book, then, is not only for pastors of churches that have a small-group ministry and laymen who are just investigating small groups for the first time. This book is also for lay leaders in charge of small-group ministries or the most nervous small-group leader. For that matter, this book is for anyone who is in a small group or is thinking about joining one. This book is about making every small group, including *your* small group, a compelling portrait of authentic biblical community and reaching as high as you can go!

Whether you've been together as a group for ten years or you're a few weeks away from your first meeting, get ready to learn easily applicable, biblical principles that can transform the relationships in your small group until it's more than you ever dreamed possible and everything God wants it to be.

Note

1. From sermon titled "Message of Faith, Gifts of Grace: Ministry In Small Groups" given by John Piper on September 20, 1998 at Bethlehem Baptist Church (www.soundofgrace.com/piper98/09-20-98.htm).

Part II
The Ascent to Intimacy

Chapter Two
Getting Ready to Make the Climb

THE STARTING POINT for closeness in your small group is relationships.

Relationships are the cornerstone of every small group. For a small group to grow into the kind of vibrant, close-knit community of believers we have been describing, members of the group will have to go through several levels of ever deepening and more meaningful relationships. The development of these types of small groups can have a powerful, transforming effect on a church because they dramatically impact the way the people in that church relate to one another. The body within the small group becomes a family not bound by blood ties but by sharing life together. Each small-group meeting becomes a family reunion, a family you will be with for eternity!

We want to share with you how this can be a reality within your small group. In the next several chapters, we will compare the journey of achieving intimacy in your small group to a mountain-climbing expedition to conquer Mount Everest.

Don't put down the book! We're not saying you have to join a super-elite climbing team to grow closer to one another or that you have to spend the incredible sums of money needed to launch an Everest expedition. But there are so many lessons you can learn about meeting challenges, climbing higher, supporting one another, and reaching great goals by looking at an elite climbing team.

We'd like to help your small groups reach higher than you've ever gone before in terms of closeness to the Lord and one another. Without a doubt, both scaling the heights of a mountain and developing intimacy in a small group can be challenging, even exhausting at times. Both require strength, endurance, and commitment. But there's also that exhilarating, exciting, and breathtaking view from the top that can make you feel more alive than you have ever felt before.

In addition, our goal is to show you how to reach the summit of intimacy in your small group, so you, in turn, can help others get there too.

Do You Have the Right Stuff?

To reach the summit on Mount Everest successfully, or to even come close, there are certain things you must have before you ever start scaling the heights. These things are not optional; they are necessities.

You need the right clothing and equipment. You need to be in peak physical and mental condition. You must have high-altitude mountaineering experience. You need an experienced guide, preferably one who has been to the summit before. You need a team of support personnel for food, water, and communications, as well as a team of Sherpas, natives of the region, to help portage your equipment from Base Camp to the camps at higher elevations. You've got to acclimate to the altitude. You need a good strategy for the climb, including how long to stay at each camp along the way, when to move on, and when to rest. Unless you are a remarkable human being, you need oxygen for the climb (fewer than a dozen Americans have reached the summit of Everest without it). It is not uncommon for it to take a full two years of preparation before you are able to attempt the climb!

Fortunately, although there are definite similarities, climbing the small-group mountain and reaching the summit of intimacy is not as physically difficult and dangerous as climbing Everest. It does take time and preparation, though, and a steely determination to reach the goal. But the goal is attainable for every small group! In fact, we are convinced that if you learn, understand, and apply the principles you learn in this book within your small group, the summit can be yours. Just as you need the right equipment for climbing Mount Everest, knowing the principles you will learn is not optional; it is a necessity.

Base Camp for Small Groups

For a climbing team, Base Camp is a time for gathering equipment and for getting to know those people your life will depend on in the days to come. For small groups, the better you get to know those in your group, the more life you'll find yourself giving and gaining as well.

For example, it is critical that you understand your own, God-given strengths from the first step into your group. God has uniquely designed you with strengths and gifts that he expects you to use in his service. Do you know what they are? Many people don't, and their effectiveness in ministry is hindered by it. Do you know the strengths and gifts of the others in your small group? If not, the development of dynamic communication and compelling relationships is hampered. How well are you able to blend the different strengths and gifts in your group?

We'll talk more in Part III about an incredibly powerful tool we encourage each person in your small group to take, called the Leading From Your Strengths™ assessment. It's a way, in less than ten minutes, to go online, take a short assessment, and then instantly be e-mailed back a twenty-eight page report on your strenths. Why is that so important? As you'll see later in this book, it can help you really see, understand, and value your own strengths and the strenghts of others in important ways.

In 1 Corinthians 12, God calls the church a "body." We're not all ears or eyes, but he did put us together by divine design! In other words, we need one another, and understanding one another is crucial to being his body!

After Base Camp, we'll be stopping at four high places, each one a stepping-stone for going even higher. These camps for small groups are centered on the four words we mentioned earlier, and they will be subjects of entire chapters to come:

- Commitment
- Honesty
- Acceptance
- Trust

All of which lead to
• Intimacy

When it comes to mountain climbing, not every expedition is guaranteed to reach the summit of Mount Everest. We know as well that not every small group will go all the way from Base Camp through every stop to the top. But we can guarantee that if you read, study, and apply the principles in this book, you will have the tools you need to reach higher than you ever have or may have thought possible.

READY FOR THE JOURNEY

To help you understand more about going higher as a small group, we're going to introduce you to a team of climbers who, in the chapters to come, will show you about teamwork and small-group closeness. Let's get to know the climbing team we'll be following to the summit.

Your expert guide is an experienced climber who has been on the summit of Everest before. His profile is top-notch:

Name: Richard Welch

Marital status: Married to Kelly

Age: 36

Children: 1 boy, age 2

Occupation: Climbing expedition leader, motivational speaker

Hometown: Pedro Bay, Alaska

Climbing experience: Began climbing in 1989 and high altitude climbing in 1991. Regularly climbs mountains all over the world. He has achieved the Seven Summits distinction by climbing the highest peaks on each continent, becoming one of only thirty-eight Americans to do so. He is considered one of the greatest technical climbers in the world. If successful, this will be his third summit of Everest.

Other interests: Hunting and waterskiing

Motto for this trip: "When you reach the summit of Everest, there is nowhere else to climb. You're on top of the world!"

In the chapters that follow, you will receive dispatches from Richard as he and his four climbing companions take on Everest. Thanks to the Internet and the advent of new technology, you will read about the expedition's experiences in almost real time.

You will get to know each of the climbers more closely at Everest Base Camp and beyond, but here is a short bio of each climber that gives you important information and insights into each person's motivation for being on this expedition:

∽

Name: Matt Cody
Marital status: Single
Age: 45
Occupation: Plaintiff's trial attorney
Hometown: New York, New York
Climbing experience: Began high-altitude climbing in 1995. Most recent summit attempt was K-2, on the border between Pakistan and China in 2003. Summit bid was unsuccessful. Last successful summit attempt was Aconcagua in Argentina in 2001. Wants summit of Everest badly.
   Other interests: Hang gliding, surfing, and extreme mountain biking
   Motto for this trip: "Go big or go home!"

∽

Name: Dan Egenolf
Marital status: Married to Jan
Children: 3 sons, ages 18, 14, and 8, and 3 daughters, ages 17, 12, and 10
Age: 43
Occupation: Chief accountant for a Fortune 500 company
Hometown: Rockport, Maine
Climbing experience: Began high-altitude climbing in 1989. Most recent successful summit was Denali in Alaska in 2003. Has reached summits on Kilamanjaro, Cho Oyu, and Aconcagua.
   Other interests: Bicycling, hockey, and sailing
   Motto for this trip: "The summit is optional, coming back alive is mandatory."

∽

Name: Jan Stevenson
Marital Status: Married to Jim
Children: None
Age: 33
Occupation: Ski instructor, search and rescue team member, part-time comedian at local nightspots
Hometown: Winter Park, Colorado
Climbing experience: Experienced ice and rock climber. This is her first major high-altitude climb.
Other interests: Fly-fishing, breeding Alaskan malamutes— even though she is allergic to dog hair
Motto for this trip: "If at first you don't succeed, destroy all evidence that you ever tried."

Name: Rob Tompson
Marital status: Married to Kim
Children: 5 boys, ages 18, 17, 15, 15 (twins), and 13
Age: 38
Occupation: Math teacher at St. Thomas Preparatory School, volunteer fireman
Hometown: Seattle, Washington
Climbing experience: Began high-altitude climbing in 1994. Reached summit of Denali in 2002 and 2003. Has seven summits of Mount Rainer in Washington state
Other interests: Waterskiing, windsurfing, and kayaking
Motto for this trip: "If I can handle five teenage boys, this should be a piece of cake."

As we follow this team throughout the book, you'll share their climb from Base Camp, up to C1, C2, C3, and C4, and you'll see how they prepare to climb the summit! Through their experience you'll learn their unique strengths and how they blend their differences into a world-class team, able to face incredible challenges and reach great heights.

THE GREATEST CLIMB OF YOUR LIFE

Every climbing team that seeks to scale Mount Everest must first journey to Katmandu, the capital of Nepal, in Southern Asia.

Katmandu is bordered by China on the north and India on the south. From Katmandu it is a spectacular thirty-minute flight to the village of Lukla, which is perched on the side of a Himalayan foothill. The takeoff and landings into Lukla are called STOLs, an acronym for Short Take Offs and Landings. Most flights are two hours late, which is actually on time for this area.

Once on the ground, climbers begin a series of hikes through different villages, which helps the team acclimate to higher and higher altitudes on their way to Base Camp. On the way they pass through forests of vibrant rhododendrons, by cliffside monasteries, and cross over several swinging bridges decorated with colorful prayer flags from hopeful climbers.

They will stop at one of the villages, like one called Sangboche, to inspect their equipment and supplies. More than fifteen hundred pounds of equipment and supplies have been helicoptered in and will be taken by yak to Everest Base Camp. The next village is Tengboche, and getting there is more challenging than they think. The final hill before Tengboche rises more than twenty-two hundred feet, and most climbers have to stop several times to catch their breath. The pace is easy to allow their red blood cells to multiply. This enables them to go higher and higher in altitude. Going too quickly now is dangerous. Many first-time trekkers going too fast develop pulmonary or cerebral edema, a swelling of the heart or brain, and are forced to turn back.

The trail to Everest Base Camp gets crowded. There are usually several expeditions headed to Base Camp, each group with their own yaks and porters. The effects of higher altitude are obvious as the team hikes into the village of Loboche, only another five hours on foot from Everest Base Camp. They are at just over sixteen thousand feet above sea level and find themselves out of breath at every hill now. And there is no shortage of hills in this place!

The team you will be following will soon reach Base Camp, which is *17,500 feet above sea level*. It will be a busy place. There will be at least twenty other teams at Base Camp, all in different stages of making a summit attempt on Everest. They will meet several times each day as a team and go on several practice climbs together so they get to know one another's climbing style and so their guide, Richard, can do his final evaluation of the skill and strength of each climber. Getting to know everyone else on the climbing team in a short period of time will be a crucial element to the success of the expedition. At any time one of the climbers may have to put his or her life in the hands of another team member during the ascent. Their knowledge of who they are and what their tendencies are, as well as their climbing ability, will give them the confidence to make that split-second decision.

YOUR GROUP'S JOURNEY

Your small group is on a journey too, to the summit of intimacy. For each of you, the journey will be different. Each stage on the way to intimacy will pose unique problems and challenges that will be more or less difficult depending on the makeup of your group. Your group may take longer on the stage of Honesty, while others may get stuck at the stage of Acceptance. Trust God to give you strength for the attempt. And trust the principles you are about to learn. They are tested and reliable and, when applied in your group, will yield good fruit.

Chapter Three
Base Camp for Your Small Group

BASE CAMP—GETTING TO KNOW YOU

THIS IS THE FIRST STEP in relationship building in your small group. You begin by investing the time it takes to get to know others in the group—their values, beliefs, styles, and attitudes. By spending time with them, you learn enough to decide to invest more in the relationship.

Expedition Guide's Dispatch

Base Camp, April 8

Everest Base Camp never ceases to amaze me. Expedition teams from all over the world come to Everest Base Camp, forming quite an eclectic community. But they are all united by a common purpose: to climb the world's tallest mountain and set foot on the top of the world. This area of rocky fields, as close to the base of the mountain as you can get and still be safe from the occasional avalanche, is always busy. It was no different when we arrived at camp this morning. The teams already here range in size from two to twenty-two, and each of them has staked out a camp with enough room for personal tents, a mess tent, and lots of food and equipment. There isn't much room left, but we found an acceptable spot between teams from Japan and Italy.

It took longer than usual to get settled because Dan was very particular about arranging all of his things in exactly the right order. We were in a hurry because the puja ceremony, in which a Buddhist priest asks the gods of the mountain for protection and permission to climb, was about to start. Everyone at Base Camp attends the puja ceremony, and no Sherpa will climb Everest without one. Since our Sherpa team is going to carry all of our heavy equipment and supplies up the mountain, I am very motivated to be there. I actually enjoy going because it takes about five hours and, instead of praying to Sagarmatha (Mother Goddess of the World), I spend that time praying for God's blessing on our climb and for each one of my climbers individually. Matt just about blew a gasket waiting for Dan to get finished, especially when Dan refolded his shirts for the third time. I will pray for patience for Matt.

I'm back. We made it to the ceremony just in time. The next few days will be spent organizing equipment and gear and acclimating to get ready for our climb. Then we will take a trip up to C1 to set up there and stow some food and equipment. The trip will give us a good chance to practice the many different climbing techniques we'll need on Everest.

We will spend the night and come back the next morning. We need to get through the Khumbu Icefalls early in the day before the sun warms up the ice. More news later.

BASE CAMP—APRIL 13

The last few days seem like a blur. We were involved in an accident in the Icefalls on our way back from C1 yesterday. No one on my team was injured, but two Sherpas from another team fell, and one had to be airlifted out by helicopter after he was carried down with the help of my team in quite a heroic effort. The Icefalls are always dangerous, with a lot of hanging ice, but the route the Sherpas built this year has fewer ladder crossings and steep vertical climbs than usual. Maybe this lulled us all into complacency.

My team had worked its way through the top of the Icefalls when there was a large ice collapse behind us. The collapse took out a ladder crossing over a nasty crevasse. Our team quickly climbed back up to help and found that half of the team making the crossing was trapped on each side of the crevasse. Luckily, the injured Sherpas were on our side. I have to say that my team reacted magnificently. Jan, who had been cracking jokes a minute before, was the first of our team to the injured Sherpa, and she immediately began working on him. She stabalized him and probably saved his life. When she began barking orders to others on our team, even Matt, who usually acts as if he is in charge, hopped to it. Matt and Dan helped other Sherpas carry the critically injured Sherpa down. It was a slow and difficult climb down, but the descent was made much easier with the extra lengths of rope Dan had in his pack that were used to belay the Sherpa in some of the tougher spots.

Today is a rest day for the team, and we will probably take off a couple more days to recover after a difficult, emotional climb down from C1. The last few days have been cool and crisp in the mornings but hotter than usual in the afternoons, so staying out of the Icefalls is a good idea anyway. I am taking stock of my team and am pleased by what I am finding out about their personalities and skills. Everyone is very different, but so far we seem to function well together.

*I sure learned a lot about Jan today. She is very funny
and quite a character. I was beginning to wonder if she could
ever take anything seriously. Her easygoing attitude toward
everything had me wondering whether she should even be
here. If you aren't serious and focused on Everest, you endanger yourself and everyone on the team. But when I saw how
well she handled an emergency situation, I lost any doubts
I had. With Jan along, we won't be short on laughter, and we
won't be lacking someone we can count on when the chips are
down. Speaking of chips, Jan challenged the rest of the team
to a chip-throwing contest. Yak chips. Yak chips are much big-
ger and much smellier than cow chips. Should be fun.*
   Richard

Moving Higher

Investing the time it takes to get to know others—their values, beliefs, styles,
and attitudes—is the first step in relationship building in your small group. By
spending time with them, you learn enough about them so you can choose
to invest more in the relationships.

BASE CAMP FOR YOUR SMALL GROUP

Perhaps the most important element of a successful attempt to
reach the summit of Mount Everest is what happens at Base Camp
before the climb ever really begins. For most expeditions this is the
critical time when the climbers really get to know one another. As
Richard learned with Jan, that information can make a big difference
on Everest.

Although it may sound simplistic, the same holds true for your
small group. At the start of any small group, it is crucial that the
members get to know one another. How well this is accomplished
can mean life and death to the group. Knowing one another is the
foundation for everything that will happen later.

If you want your small group to be successful in things such as
spiritual growth, service to others, and evangelism later on, you
must build a base of understanding with one another as the group
begins. If you want to successfully navigate your way through the

stages that a small group must go through to reach intimacy, you must prepare in advance. Authentic biblical community simply cannot happen unless the difficult groundwork of "getting to know you" has occurred. This is a crucial step for group leaders. You simply can't lead or shepherd people whom you don't know. And no one in your small group can minister to the needs of people they don't know. Without this foundation, many groups find themselves stuck at a superficial level from which they never escape.

Do You Recognize Me?

Getting to know the people in your small group sounds like an easy task, but it is surprising how difficult this step can be. Many group leaders try, but they inevitably meet resistance. When they do, their tendency is to skip this step or do it halfheartedly. There are many reasons this happens, but the primary reason is common to all of us. We are all great fakers.

Think about your relationship with your next-door neighbors. Not the neighbors just down the street or the ones a few blocks over, but the ones right next door. The ones you see every week taking out the trash or doing yard work or just driving in and out of the driveway. How well do you know them? Odds are that you don't know them very well. You are friendly with them, but are you a friend or merely an acquaintance? You may even have several conversations a week, but does your interaction with them ever reach a personal level? Are they real, authentic, "where the rubber meets the road" conversations? Do you share any of the secret places of your life with them? Usually not.

There once was a woman who had a near-death experience while on the operating table. She saw God and asked him if this was her time to die. He assured her that she had another twenty-six years, four months, and nineteen days to live. When she came out of anesthesia, she remembered what God had promised her. She decided to make the most of her newfound longevity, so she underwent a whole series of cosmetic surgeries.

She got liposuction, a face-lift, a tummy tuck, the whole works. She even changed her hair color, got colored contact lenses, and bought a completely new wardrobe. After making her final purchase, she hurried out of the store. She was admiring her new look in the store window when she stepped off the curb in front of a speeding taxi and was killed. When she got up to heaven, she immediately went to God and asked, "What happened? You told me I had another twenty-six years to live." God replied, "Sorry, I didn't recognize you."

We construct a barrier and maintain it, making the job of getting to know us difficult, if not impossible. This barrier is the image we project to others. Some call it the mask we wear. In any event, it's a facade or "false front" that inhibits anyone else from knowing who we truly are. We all have one, to a greater or lesser degree, because it is a condition common to man. Adam and Eve started with a simple fig leaf, and we have been covering our true selves ever since. This is why we can live right next door to people for years and never really know them. And this is why we can go to church and worship with the same body of believers for years and never really know them either.

It isn't just the existence of the facade that makes the job of knowing us harder, although the walls some people build around themselves are very thick and high. It's also the effect the facade has on us that magnifies the problem. In their excellent book *TrueFaced*, Bill Thrall, Bruce McNicol, and John Lynch describe it this way:

> Hiding drains us. When we hide we can never rest. We live every waking moment with a nagging fear that someone or something will blow our cover. Hiding requires constant vigilance and maintenance. Our masks are made of papier-mâché, remember? Good material for fashioning a new look in a hurry, but get it wet and, badda-bing, we're looking like our uncle Floyd after a face tuck! Things start to get distorted quickly. We can't stay out in public too long because we're in constant need of repair. We need a lot of down time. After a while, we can't remember what the mask looked like the last time we put it on.[1]

BREAKING DOWN THE WALLS

How can we get to know others when we are consumed with hiding ourselves? Where do we get the energy to invest in relationships when we spend it all making ourselves look good? What can break down the barriers that make it hard for others to see the truth about us? The best answer to these questions is God's perfect love. God's love is unconditional. It is the most complete love we can ever know. In fact, in our humanness, it is difficult to comprehend the extent of God's love. But if we rest in his love, we can find the strength to take down our facade and we can help others do the same.

"Just as the Father has loved Me, I have also loved you; abide in My love. . . . This is My commandment, that you love one another just as I have loved you" (John 15: 9, 12). Consider the eternal progression of God's love. God loves his Son, Jesus loves us, and we in turn are to love one another. God loves his Son who is most worthy, and Jesus loves us who are most unworthy. God's love empowered and sustained his Son. Christ's love empowers and sustains us. We, in turn, have the ability to love one another just as God made us, to empower others to take down the facade and sustain them in revealing their true selves. Because Christ's love flows through us, we can love our brothers and sisters not just in word but also in deed. Our love for others can become a lifestyle, a continual process of considering others as more important than ourselves.

Before we come to know Christ's love, the truth about our sinfulness and just how far that separates us from a holy God is veiled to us. When we accept Christ as Savior, our understanding of that same sin, in relationship to God's holiness, begins to grow. But we still hide the truth from others and ourselves. We rationalize our behavior, desperately trying to bridge the gap between what we know of God's holiness and our increasing awareness of our sinfulness. At some point we come to the end of ourselves, and God has us cornered. There is no other place to run but into his loving embrace. Only then can we accept the painful truth about ourselves. Only then can God's love cover the multitude of our sins. And this love, if it is active in our hearts and lives, enables us to tear down the facade we have built around ourselves, and we can help our brothers and sisters do the same so we can achieve intimacy in our relationships. Only the power of God's love is strong enough to do it.

TIME IS OF THE ESSENCE

Even when God's love works in us to accept our true selves and we can begin revealing that to others, there is another necessary element for which there is no substitute. That element is time. Time together in fellowship, both spontaneous and planned. Time to learn other people's strengths and weaknesses. Time to build the trust upon which a relationship stands. This is not just busywork. We are far too busy to spend time together without a purpose. We need to intentionally build meaningful, significant relationships. Shared experiences with people in your small groups are one of the best ways to achieve this purpose.

Most small-group experts suggest that it takes six to twelve months for a group to begin to gel. Not all groups make it that long before they break up for various reasons, but for those who stay the course, the reward is sweet. They are on the path to intimacy. There is no substitute for time spent together, getting past the doing and getting to the being.

A TOOL THAT CAN HELP YOU TAKE A QUANTUM LEAP TOWARD UNDERSTANDING AND CLOSENESS

There's a tool we'd like to introduce to you that your small group can use to make a quantum leap in getting to know one another. This is true whether your group has met only a few times or you are a group of grizzled small-group veterans. This online tool is the Leading From Your Strengths™ assessment.

This assessment is taken online from any computer and, within eight to ten minutes, each member in your small group will receive a twenty-eight-page report that explains who they really are, without the facade. Spend just one small-group session going through the highlights of each person's report, and the relational equity in your group will be at an all-time high. Better yet, have your small group go through the four-week Small Group Study found in Part III of this book. Either way, the assessment is a fun, informative way to build deeper relationships quickly. You'll find out more about the Leading From Your Strengths™ assessment in Part III.

Bill Hybels, senior pastor of Willow Creek Church, has said, "Real, authentic community can't be microwaved. It takes hard work and sometimes hand-to-hand combat to get people into groups and then to experience transformational community."[2] Part of the hard work is getting to know one another. The most important time for a small group is the time *between* meetings. What happens during these times determines whether the group will move on toward intimacy.

Notes

1. Bill Thrall, Bruce McNicol, and John Lynch, *TrueFaced: Trust God and Others With Who You Really Are* (Colorado Springs, Colo.: NavPress, 2003), 60.

2. From "Nuggets from Small Groups Conference" quoted by Bill Hybels at the National Small Group Conference at Willow Creek Church (http://smallgroups.com/secure/dynamics/062000news/nuggetsp.html). Copyright 2000 by smallgroups.com.

Chapter Four

Commitment—the First Steps toward the Summit

STARTING AT C1—COMMITMENT

FELLOWSHIP TOGETHER in a small group requires commitment. It is the foundation upon which deeper relationships are built. Without commitment, your small group will be just like any other group you belong to. Your small group should be different. Commitment is what makes your small group different from your dinner club or playgroup.

EXPEDITION GUIDE'S DISPATCH

CAMP 1, APRIL 18

We are still at C1 today. Our plan after coming from Base Camp yesterday was to stay one night and then go on to C2 for several nights. We have spent the last week acclimating by alternating between Base Camp and C1, as well as making one overnight stay at C2 to finish setting up our camp there. As always, the key to acclimating is not how long you stay at a certain altitude but making lots of transitions from higher altitudes to lower altitudes and back. We have two large tents with a cook and lots of food at C2 now. Our Sherpas will have most of the oxygen and equipment there in the next few days. We will use C2 as our staging camp for trips higher up.

We woke up before five to start up but soon changed our minds as strong winds and heavy snow started coming in. We only got about three inches of snow, but the heavy winds kept coming. We hope to try again tomorrow, but forecasts say the high winds might continue. We are still on track for a summit attempt in mid-May, which has historically offered the best climbing conditions.

CAMP 1, APRIL 19

The wind here at C1 has not let up. If anything, the weather has deteriorated with heavy gray clouds and snow showers moving in. C4 had six inches of fresh snow this morning. It looks as if no one will be moving on the mountain today. If we can't get up to C2 tomorrow, we will have to go back to Base Camp for a day or two at lower altitude before we try again.

Dan did not sleep well last night. He woke up several times having trouble breathing. He is complaining of a headache that just won't go away. I'm concerned because these are some of the symptoms of mountain sickness. If his condition persists, we will have to get him back to Base Camp. Matt has already expressed concerns to me about whether Dan's condition would cause our climb to C2 to be canceled and delay our acclimating process. I need to talk with Jan and Rob about this before we make a decision.

CAMP 1, APRIL 20

Dan is getting worse, and we are packing up to get back down to Base Camp. Dan's face is swollen, and he is nauseous. He has mountain sickness and needs the thicker air at Base Camp to recover. Our team discussed sending Dan back to Base Camp with a couple of our Sherpas so we could go up to C2. Matt was in favor of going up without Dan. He was concerned with how any delay would affect our overall schedule. Jan was on the fence. However, Rob gave a spirited defense of staying together as a team and not leaving Dan. Rob made the point forcefully that this could have happened to any one of us, that all of us will need help at some time on the mountain, and the team is obligated to be there for one another. In the short time I have known Rob, he has shown himself to be fiercely loyal, and that came through as he convinced Matt and Jan to stick together as a team.

We're doing the right thing, but I was glad not to have to be the heavy and demand it. I've seen many teams that didn't ever have the commitment to one another that my team showed today. Many climbers have an "I am an island" philosophy. That philosophy has often proved fatal on Everest. I hope the spirit of loyalty and commitment Rob inspired continues to infect the team because Rob is right about one thing: we will all need help sometime, somewhere on the mountain, and we need to know we will be there for one another.

Richard

Moving Higher

Fellowship together in a small group requires commitment. It is the foundation upon which deeper relationships are built. Without commitment your small group will be just like any other group you belong to. Your small group should be different. Commitment is what makes your small group different from your dinner club or playgroup.

How Bad Do We Want It?

Relationship.

Community.

Intimacy.

These are important words. They should not be used lightly because when they are overused, they lose their meaning. In the preceding chapter, we used these words a lot. We intended for them to be full of meaning. We dared to suggest that God's people could have relationships with one another that lead to true intimacy. We implied that with God's love working in and through us, and by spending perhaps our most precious resource, time, on building into the lives of others, real community is established. Real community leads to true intimacy. Now, we may have lost some of you right there. Some of you may think that, at best, we are being too optimistic and, at worst, we are dreaming the impossible dream. Can any of us really have true intimacy in *any* of our relationships, let alone the relationships in our small group?

We aren't saying you will have intimacy with everyone in your small group. But we are boldly saying that you can have intimacy with some of them. Developing intimacy is hard work, but it is not an impossible dream. Still, many people simply can't imagine having those kinds of relationships. Lynn was one of those people.

Lynn was skeptical when she first heard the principles behind Leading From Your Strengths™ and took our assessment. Lynn's best friend in her small group was Karen, but even though they had known each other for six years, their relationship wasn't intimate. They weren't committed to each other. That's because Lynn didn't trust Karen. Early in their relationship, Lynn, on several occasions, shared with Karen some personal and private information about her marriage. Each time she did, she found out that Karen had subsequently shared the information with other people. Karen ostensibly did this to help Lynn by asking others to pray for her. But eventually Lynn stopped believing Karen had pure motives and saw no justification for Karen's betraying her confidences. She vowed never to share anything beyond the superficial with Karen again. Karen didn't seem to notice and thought her relationship with Lynn was great. Lynn was saddened by the whole affair. She loved everything else about Karen, but this particular character flaw of Karen's stopped the growth of their friendship dead in its tracks. Lynn despaired of its ever changing.

We met with Lynn after she took our assessment to discuss her report, and she told us the story of her relationship with Karen. Although she desired it greatly, she simply couldn't believe our assurances that we could help her break through this barrier and grow in her relationship with Karen. She told us exactly what you might be thinking: *I don't believe I can have intimacy with anyone.*

Ironically, Lynn's strengths were virtually identical to Karen's! Their reports showed them both as being extremely friendly, outgoing, and enthusiastic. And both of them loved and needed people. They both desperately needed a best friend. However, we soon discovered in talking with Lynn that she was a classic people pleaser. Her biggest fear was causing a strain in any important relationship and losing the approval of that person. This proved to be the reason she would not confront Karen with her failure to keep a confidence. We finally convinced Lynn that she had to move out of her comfort zone and do the hard things that true friends do for each other. Lynn realized that if she really loved Karen, she had to confront her. Her goal was to help Karen become the person God wanted her to be, and Lynn knew God wanted to use her as one of his instruments to do it. The confrontation was difficult, even traumatic, given both women's anxiety over offending each other, but it produced repentance, forgiveness, and restoration. And it cleared the way for them to share each other's lives in such a way that today their relationship can only be characterized as intimate and committed.

Intimacy can happen, if we want it badly enough. It's not always an easy process, but God is in the business of transforming people and relationships. God is at work in his people's lives, and we need to be involved in the process as he changes them.

Because He First Loved Us

In John 15:12–13, Jesus does no less than command the disciples to love one another, to be willing to die for one another. Then in verse 14 he says, "You are my friends if you do what I command you." And just in case they (or we) don't get it, he repeats the command to love one another in verse 17. These verses illustrate what the disciples' relationships with one another were to look like.

Those relationships were to be marked by unconditional love. The disciples wanted to obey Jesus' command, not out of fear of correction or discipline, but out of a love for Jesus that resulted from his first loving them. We should have the same motivation today.

During his earthly ministry Jesus chose his disciples and molded them into a band of brothers through deep, committed relationships. Jesus took them in their lowly, sinful condition and created them into a small group of men whose lives became a reflection of their Master. What changed them was Christ's commitment to them. He chose these particular men out of the world and committed to sharing his life with them. He gave to them freely of his love and his time. He knew that the way to reach the multitudes was to invest in the lives of these few. Indeed, these few changed the world! And the early church followed the example of commitment to others that Jesus established. The church in Acts set a pretty high standard; they met every day (Acts 2:46; 5:42). And you just can't meet every day together and not be an integral part of one another's lives.

Your small group may not interact every day, but each person in your group can follow Christ's example and give others the same thing Christ gave his disciples, love and time. All of the people in your small group must commit to sharing their lives with one another so that no one stands alone; everyone cares and is cared for. A small group should be more than just a group arranged around some affinity, such as mothers of young children or guys who like to play golf. Neither is a small group just another Sunday school class or Bible study, even though there is the teaching and study of God's Word. And small groups should resist becoming simply a recovery group or group therapy, even though members in the group care for one another and meet one another's needs. Instead, small groups should be in the process of developing deep, committed relationships. This accomplishes an eternal purpose, the building up of the body of Christ. But this kind of genuine fellowship requires commitment.

COMMITMENT TO WHAT?

The commitment we are talking about is first a commitment to God. As we said before, all people have a universal need for a vertical relationship with God. Just as with the tower of Babel (Gen. 11), any undertaking by man to create community apart from God will utterly fail.

Second, commitment to other believers is required. We also have a built-in need for horizontal relationships. But our need for human fellowship is frustrated by our sinful nature. We resist open, accountable relationships because we would rather operate in secret. Yet when the transforming blood of Christ saves us, we gain the ability through the power now at work within us to reconcile relationships and enjoy true fellowship with other believers. Christ is our Savior, but he also is the Restorer of our relationships that, without Christ's intervention, would remain irreparably damaged. "Therefore do not be partakers with them; for you were formerly darkness, but now you are Light in the Lord; walk as children of Light" (Eph. 5:7–8).

Third, in the context of small groups, commitment to the group is necessary. Intimacy in relationships is not exclusive to small groups. But once a small group is established, intimacy should be a stated goal. It is difficult to achieve this goal, however, unless everyone in the boat is pulling on the oars in the same direction. Otherwise, you are simply rowing around in circles.

The success of any small group is measured by the commitment of its members to be the body of Christ for one another. How would you respond to someone in a small group who said, "I love the group, and I wouldn't trade it for the world." This sounds good, but it reflects a lack of commitment by the person saying it. How much better does it sound if you hear, "I love *my* group, and I wouldn't trade it for the world." That simple change of emphasis makes all the difference. That kind of commitment to the group changes lives within it.

WHAT'S IN IT FOR ME?

Until you are committed, you always have the chance to walk away. That's exactly why most people choose never to commit fully. *They* always *hold back* some part of themselves so they have an escape hatch if things don't turn out the way they want them to. This hesitancy to commit is the silent killer of many relationships. And it can kill your small group.

Much like commitment in the marriage relationship, commitment to others in your small group needs to be covenantal. A covenant is a binding agreement between two or more parties. Similarly, covenantal commitment is one that binds people to one another. A marriage covenant is supposed to mean one man and one woman for life. Unfortunately, whether you look at statistics on marriage Christian or secular, this definition applies to only about half of them. Why? Because many people make a decision to get married but never make a commitment to their spouse. There is a big difference between the two. The same is true of the church today. Many people have made a decision for Christ but have never made a commitment to him. So they call themselves Christians, but they choose not to go to church, or, if they do, they never give of their time, treasure, and talent. No wonder the impact of the church on our society at large seems minimal.

The apostle Paul pleads with us to be people of commitment. "Therefore I urge you, brethren, by the mercies of God, to present your bodies a living and holy sacrifice, acceptable to God, which is your spiritual service of worship" (Rom. 12:1). Paul tells us we are to be "living sacrifices" with the understanding that there is no halfway sacrifice or commitment. Commitment is not a dial; it is a switch. It is either on or off. You are either committed or not.

The story of the pig and the chicken illustrates the point. One day the pig and the chicken were walking down the road. They saw a sign in front of a church saying that there was a breakfast to feed the poor the next morning. "We should donate a ham-and-egg breakfast to help the poor," suggested the chicken. "That is a generous offer," replied the pig, "but you are asking much more from me than you are willing to give yourself. For what you are willing to give is a contribution, but for me it is total commitment!" Many of us are willing to give something of ourselves like the chicken. Far fewer are willing to give what was asked of the pig—total commitment.

If your small group is going to thrive and relationships blossom, total commitment is essential—at least relationally. Members have to be willing, for example, to confront others when they offend them rather than withdrawing from the relationship. They have to be willing to abide by the decision of the majority when they are in the minority, without quitting. They have to be willing to give sacrificially of their time when someone needs them instead of choosing not to be inconvenienced. Everyone in the group needs to have the confidence to speak their minds and be themselves without fear of rejection or causing others to leave. Members in your small group should feel a sense of obligation to others in the group that constrains their impulse to quit when the going gets tough. Their commitment should compel them to stay.

WE NEED TO COMMIT, BUT HOW?

William Booth, founder of the Salvation Army, once declared, "The greatness of a man's power is the measure of his surrender." This is true in the context of commitment. The strength of one's commitment is directly related to the extent of his surrender to God. When we are intentionally, purposefully yielded to God and his will, we can commit with our whole heart, with confidence and trust.

The word *surrender* is not popular in our culture because it suggests weakness and defeat. But as with many other truths in Scripture, what the world thinks of as foolish, God has established as wise. If you have ever seen your children playing "mercy," you know it is a game in which you lock hands with your opponent and try to bend his hands back at the wrist until he gives up. The object is total, unconditional surrender. That is what God wants from us, although he does not accept forced surrender. But if we are willing and if we yield ourselves, our reward is great.

In fact, total surrender is the only way to find real meaning in life. We desperately desire peace, joy, contentment, and fulfillment in our lives. We try to achieve them in so many ways—careers, money, possessions, religion, and the list goes on. But God says the only way to get these things is to give up everything. "If anyone wishes to come after Me, he must deny himself, and take up his cross and follow Me. For whoever wishes to save his life will lose it; but whoever loses his life for My sake will find it" (Matt. 16:24–25). "So then, none of you can be My disciple who does not give up all his own possessions" (Luke 14:33). God may never *require* you to give up everything to follow him, but you must be *willing* to.

The greatest benefit of living the surrendered life is that we become empty of ourselves and full of Christ. "But whatever things were gain to me, those things I have counted as loss for the sake of Christ. More than that, I count all things to be loss in view of the surpassing value of knowing Christ Jesus my Lord, for whom I have suffered the loss of all things, and count them but rubbish so that I may gain Christ" (Phil. 3:7–8). He provides the only power we have to live a committed life. We have to be surrendered to him if we want to be prepared for commitment. Challenge the people in your small group to live this way. Pray for them and with them about fully surrendering their lives to God. And you will see a group of people committed to God, committed to others, and committed to your group.

Chapter Five
Honesty—the Second High Place for Your Small Group

MOVING UP TO C2—HONESTY

COMMITMENT SETS THE STAGE for going beyond the superficial in your small group. Honesty is what drives your group into deeper relationships with one another. We must commit to be honest about ourselves, and that includes being honest with others in our small group about who we really are.

Senior Guide's Dispatch

Camp 2, April 23

It is great to be at C2. Pushing higher on the mountain gives everyone a sense of accomplishment. It is colder at almost twenty-one thousand feet, but the winds have died down considerably; and when the sun shines through the clouds, the temperatures climb rapidly. For now we are trying to stay warm in our tents as we wait for dinner. Tonight is the big burrito bash. Our Sherpa cook staff makes fantastic food, especially considering where we are.

Tomorrow is a rest day. As with any rest day, entertainment is a top priority. We may watch a movie on my laptop or play another game of Monopoly. Today we held a round-table on different topics, including politics. This could have been a disaster as I sensed there was a wide divergence of opinions on the subject. Thankfully, the lack of oxygen up here dulls your wits, so no one was able to hold forth for long and stay coherent. It was funny to see how this affected Matt. He got really mad at himself as he fumbled over a few words, and that made everyone laugh!

Camp 2, April 24

We got some bad news about Dan's father this morning. Dan got an e-mail from his brother that their dad was in the hospital undergoing emergency surgery to repair a blocked artery. Another e-mail confirmed that he came through surgery fine but was going to have a rough recovery. His situation is complicated because he has been on blood thinners for several months. This makes the recovery time a lot more dangerous than usual. His brother told him it would be touch and go for the next week or so.

Dan has spent most of the day alone in his tent. He is the most solitary member of the group anyway, but it is hard to see someone isolate himself when all you want to do is help. Dan has a difficult decision before him, whether to get home to be with his mother and abandon his summit bid or keep going. We all want to support him in any way we can, but he is not cooperating. All of us have tried to engage him in a conversation at different times this afternoon, but he told us he needs time alone.

As I write this, it is late (10 P.M.) for me to be awake. We usually have lights out here well before now. Dan is still packing for his trip back to Base Camp tomorrow. As usual, it is a job that takes him forever because of how meticulous he is. He still hasn't spoken to anyone more than to say he is leaving in the morning. Our sidar, Lakpa Temba, and another Sherpa volunteer will accompany him. Say a prayer for Dan with me tonight.

CAMP 2, APRIL 25

My apologies for not getting this communication out to you sooner. Last night was my second night in a row of being up late, and the lack of sleep together with the lack of oxygen is taking its toll. It has been another great day at C2, although this one was better than most. First let me tell you that Dan is still with us. The story of how this came about will take a little longer.

I woke up this morning, very early I might add, to the sound of three noisy people right outside my tent. I wasn't even out of my sleeping bag when Jan, Rob, and Matt burst into my tent. The three of them talked last night and decided that they weren't going to let Dan leave without talking first. They weren't really asking my permission as much as they were inviting me to participate. I agreed and went to wake Dan up while the three amigos went to the mess tent to wait for us.

Dan was already awake (and still packing!) when I got to his tent. I asked him if he wanted some breakfast, and he followed me to the mess tent. When he saw the others waiting for him, he gave me a look as if I had betrayed him, but I just smiled as he took a seat at the table. Matt, in his unique "sensitive as a steam roller" style, confronted Dan with his decision to leave without talking to them. Dan simply lowered his head in silence. He looked up, and tears were streaming down his face. Then he let loose, and his feelings rushed out like water when a dam bursts. He told us how he struggled his whole life with being good enough to win his dad's approval. He said his father never showed him any physical or emotional affection, and he was never close to his father, even as an adult. He wanted to stay but felt an obligation to be with his father.

*If that wasn't amazing enough, Matt got teary eyed and
told a similar story about his relationship with his father. Jan
and Rob stared at Matt with mouths open as he shared intimate details of his life with his father. Matt even gave Dan a
(very short) hug. Dan thought about it for a few minutes and
then told us he had decided to stay. His brother had challenged Dan to stay promising that he would look after his
father while Dan pursued the dream of a lifetime. Besides, Jan
added, Dan was winning in Monopoly and couldn't leave now.*

*Later Dan told us he couldn't thank us enough for forcing
him to talk. We told him how courageous it was to be that
open and honest with relative strangers. He admitted it was
always difficult for him to open up but it would be easier from
now on. Wow! Another exciting, exhausting day on "the Big
E." Time for bed. Good-night and thanks for your prayers
last night. They worked!*

Richard

Moving Higher

Commitment sets the stage for going beyond the superficial in your small
group. Honesty is what drives your group into deeper relationships with one
another. We must commit to be honest about ourselves, and that includes
being honest with others in our small group about who we really are.

CAN I GET A WITNESS?

The packed courtroom buzzes with anticipation. Everyone is
talking to someone sitting near by. The judge's arrival is announced,
and a hush falls over the crowd as he enters. The judge nods at the
prosecutor. The prosecutor stares at the defendant as he calls out a
name. A man from the crowd stands and works his way toward the
front of the room. He, too, looks in the direction of the defendant
but quickly looks away when the plaintiff meets his gaze. The man
then fixes his eyes on the prosecutor. The prosecutor gives him a
confident smile. The prosecutor knows that the information the
man is about to reveal will seal the fate of the defendant. He stands
at the front of the room, places his left hand on the Bible, and raises
his right hand. Before judge and jury, he swears, with God's help, to
"tell the whole truth and nothing but the truth."

This man is a witness. His sworn duty is to tell the truth with no amplification, alteration, or dilution. The jury will interpret the law, and the judge will apply it, but the witness is concerned only with telling the truth. If he does more or less, the outcome is tainted. If he speaks only the truth, justice can be done.

As Christians, we are witnesses too. Our Judge is unseen but ever present. The jury is the world around us. Jesus calls us as witnesses, and our duty is to tell the truth. We tell it not only with our mouths but also with our lives. Unlike the man described above, who will step down from the witness chair when he is finished testifying, we never do. Because until our life on Earth is over, we never cease to testify. For us, court is always in session, and we are always under oath. Dishonesty, deceit, fraud, deception—none of these things should have a place in our lives. We should strive to be honest and transparent. We should be real, just as Jesus was.

And perhaps the best place to learn, model, and be encouraged to deal with truth is in a small group. *Honesty is the next level your small group should strive to reach.*

THE TRUTH ABOUT US

Jesus is the living embodiment of truth (John 14:6). His life was honest and transparent. He never faked it. He never hid behind a facade. He was real (1 Pet. 2:21–22). All that he said and did was truth. His standard of honest living is the one we should strive for in our own lives and in our relationships with others. He was the perfect witness of the truth.

We know that we are far from perfect. This is why it is so difficult for us to be people of truth, living honest, transparent lives. The standard that Jesus represents is high and contrasts greatly with the truth about us. The truth about us is that we are desperately wicked sinners. Our heart's natural desires are opposed to the truth found in Christ. Even as redeemed people, we struggle with our sin nature. Our sin nature still wages war within us (Rom. 7:23). When we see the chasm between who Christ is and who we are, we are often undone.

Like Adam and Eve when they first became aware of their sin, our first instinct, when we are confronted with our own sin, is to hide. We hide from ourselves and from others. Especially others. *No one else can find out our true condition.* We don't feel righteous before

God, but we will do anything to *appear* righteous before others. So we begin building the facade.

A marriage is struggling because the husband works too much and doesn't make his wife a priority. But the couple pretends nothing is wrong, especially while they are at church or with their Christian friends. The foundation of the façade is laid. The same couple is angered and frustrated by a rebellious teenage son. But everyone outside the family thinks their son is a wonderful, mature Christian young man because he is a leader in the youth group. Another layer of the facade is carefully laid. Money is tight, and the couple is going deeper and deeper in debt. But there are the Jones to keep up with, so money is spent on a new car, extravagant vacations, and clothes from the trendiest stores. The facade grows higher. Eventually the couple begins to believe in the facade they have created. They give themselves over to the deceitful image they have made for themselves and ignore the fact that one day they will reap what they sow. It seems easier than being honest.

Our only recourse when we can't face the truth about our sin is to justify ourselves, struggling to get and keep our own righteousness. The struggle is as old as the human race. When confronted with their sin, Eve blamed the serpent, and Adam blamed God for giving him Eve. We have been trying to achieve our own righteousness ever since.

Jesus is at the end of all our attempts to achieve righteousness. But we can only see this when we get our focus off of our sin and onto him. We need to be honest about ourselves, but if we want to be free to live honest and transparent lives, we must concentrate on who Christ is and what he did for us.

If we know him and trust him as Lord and Savior, that can free us and give us the courage to be people of truth. We are justified by faith in Christ, and we have peace with God as a result (Rom. 5:1). Our justification is a one-time act in which God not only declares us not guilty, but he declares us righteous. By faith in Christ, his righteousness is credited to us, and our sin is imputed to him (2 Cor. 5:21). This is commonly called The Great Exchange, and through it, our record of sin is permanently replaced with Christ's record of sinless perfection. God no longer has any anger toward us because his wrath for our sin was completely poured out on Jesus and satisfied.

This is our position with God, but many of us stubbornly refuse to live as if it's true. Instead, we live as if we can achieve, through our own good works, what God already freely gives us. We struggle in vain to convince everyone around us that we are righteous on our own, when righteousness is only ours through the grace and mercy of God.

Have you ever seen a family building sand castles on the beach? Watch the mother or father help their child try to save the sand castle when the ocean tide rushes in. Walls are fortified and trenches are dug, but to no avail. The futility of our struggle to justify ourselves is like trying to stop the ocean waves from overcoming our sand castle. Jesus provides the only relief from the struggle. He atoned for our sin and purchased our perfection in God's eyes with his redeeming blood.

Walter Anderson, former editor of *Parade* magazine, once said, "Our lives improve only when we take chances—and the first and most difficult risk we can take is to be honest with ourselves."[1] What can you do? You can give up! End the struggle of trying to be what you are not. Admit the truth about your sin and lay it at the foot of the cross. "Let him who boasts, boast in the Lord" (1 Cor. 1:31). As we grow in our faith, we grow in our understanding of our sinful nature. But we also need to grow in our understanding of our identity in Christ. Our position is that we stand with Christ, clothed with his righteousness. We need to claim that position every day and accept and embrace what God has done for us. We are justified!

WHAT HONESTY MEANS TO THE BODY OF CHRIST AND TO YOUR SMALL GROUP

Our position with God is settled. He sees us as perfect, and in heaven we will experience that perfection. But here on earth we remain imperfect and flawed. We share this condition with every other believer, so there is no reason for judgment, moralism, or legalism. There is every reason for grace and mercy to abound. With the help of the Holy Spirit, we must walk together in Christian love, striving to keep our focus, and the focus of those walking with us, on our position with God rather than our sin. This is the foundation of true Christian community and enables us to live honest, open lives before one another.

Now more than ever we need this kind of love. We can't function as the body of Christ anymore by simply going to a service on Sunday, listening to Christian radio in the car, and reading the latest in Christian fiction. We live in days of great stress on our lives as time flies by and we exhaust ourselves with day-to-day demands, never having time for what is really important. With all this going on, how can we possibly devote time and energy to developing and nurturing close Christian relationships? The cost of doing so has never been higher. But remember the saying, "No pain, no gain." The cost in terms of time, effort, patience, prayer, humility, caring, and love is great, but so is the reward. The greatest value in this kind of love comes when people need it the most. The love and encouragement of a fellow believer on the Christian journey can be invaluable. If you have ever needed it and received it, you know!

Hebrews 10:24 exhorts us to "consider how to stimulate one another to love and good deeds." The tendency for our love for God to grow cold is not uncommon to any of us, especially when we encounter trials and tribulations or go through suffering. And when we regard one another as the same, human beings with similar weaknesses and faults, redeemed by the blood of Christ and partakers of the grace and mercy from God, we should desire to use the motivating power of love to encourage one another. Our love for others can fan the flame of love for God in someone else's heart. We can give one another the hope and confidence that God is for us and, if we trust him, he will meet our every need. We can give this gift of hope to one another, even when it is inconvenient or costly.

But none of this can happen if we are hiding behind a façade. It can happen only when we take off our masks and reveal who we truly are. This is a bold, risky move. Being honest and transparent also means being vulnerable. This is at once both attractive and frightening. It is attractive because it results in freedom—freedom from trying to appear sinless, freedom from expectations, and freedom from guilt when we fail. But living honestly is also frightening because you are giving others the ability to hurt you.

This is where your small group can play such a vital role in helping to bring change into people's lives by giving them a safe place to be honest and vulnerable. Your small group must be a place where people can expose the reality of their hearts and lives to a few trusted believers. Your small group must provide a circle of protection for people who dare to step from behind the facade and walk out into the light. Your small group must become a constant reminder of the fact that God loves us despite our continuing sin by showing others grace and mercy, even when they don't deserve it. Living an honest, transparent life amid a group of other people trying their best to do the same thing is risky, but the rewards are worth the risk.

HOW TO LOSE YOUR MASK

Of the thousands of testimonials we have received from people who have taken the Leading From Your Strengths™ assessment and read their report, the most common response we get is some variation of "This is really me!" When people take the Leading From Your Strengths™ assessment and spend time together discussing their reports, things can get really interesting. Some people are so good at masking who they really are that it takes an assessment, an objective third party if you will, to remove the mask. For many, reading the report of a good friend or spouse may be the first time they fully understand who the other person is.

This was particularly true for one couple in a small group we worked with. They owned a Christian bookstore, and both of them worked full-time in the business. Rick was outgoing and always seemed to have a smile on his face. He was easygoing and quick with the one-liners. Robin was more serious but was pleasant enough once you got to know her. She was most expressive when she was voicing her opinion. She never let an opportunity go by to let others know what it was. The others in the group simply laughed it off. Rick and Robin clearly loved each other, and the general consensus was that they were happily married.

The leader of this small group had an occasion to take the Leading From Your Strengths™ assessment. He was impressed with the results and asked the other couples in the group to take the assessment. The group leader encouraged each couple to spend some time discussing their reports as couples before group discussion. Over the next two weeks, the members of this small group watched as Rick changed before their eyes from being happy and winsome to grumpy and short tempered, without any explanation. All attempts to get under the surface and find out why met with a response that everything was "fine."

The group leader met with Rick for a heart-to-heart. Rick finally admitted that the last two weeks were the worst of his eighteen-year marriage. Rick told his leader that both he and Robin thought they were happily married, but after going through their reports together, they discovered significant issues between them that had never been addressed before.

The crux of the problem was the way they interacted at work. Her report showed Robin to be aggressive with a strong desire to do things the right way. Basically, she was controlling and made every major decision at the store. When it came to the business, there was one way, and it was her way. Rick's report showed him to be a people person and extremely trusting. Unlike Robin, he was passive when confronting a problem or challenge. But despite his easygoing and laid-back style, he strongly resented Robin's approach. He was intelligent and business savvy with ideas of his own, but Robin expressed her opinions so forcefully that his ideas were always drowned out. But the mask he had fashioned for himself was thick, and Robin had no idea the effect she was having on her husband. Even Rick had no idea how much he resented her until they shared their reports.

Their small group rallied around them, and less than a month later the old Rick was back. The intervening time had been a struggle for this couple, but eventually they were able to understand each other in a way they hadn't before. Robin was able to see Rick's strengths and appreciate that he could be a valuable asset to their business. In fact, they instituted several changes at the store because of Rick's ideas, and store traffic shot up noticeably. Rick was able to affirm his wife's God-given strengths of aggressive problem solving and getting things done. He knew the business wouldn't be nearly as successful without her efforts, and he made sure she knew it.

This type of change, though perhaps not as dramatic, occurs every day with people who take our assessment. That's why we encourage you to take the Leading From Your Strengths™ assessment and see the difference it can make for you and your small group.

Unmasking ourselves is a key to developing intimacy in small groups. The worst place you can be is feeling alone and isolated, especially when you are part of a small group. Small groups are meant to be so much more. Being honest and transparent opens the door to your life so others can come in and walk through life with you.

Note
1. Quote from www.worldofquotes.com/author/Walter-Anderson/1/.

Chapter Six

Acceptance—a Difficult Move Up the Mountain

★ ★

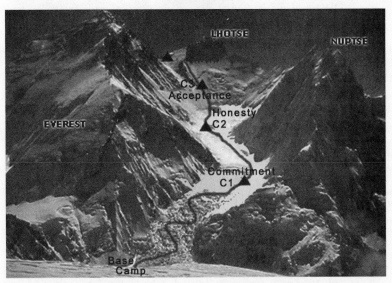

GETTING TO C3—ACCEPTANCE

ACCEPTANCE IS THE NEXT STEP after commitment and honesty, but it is not an easy step to make. It is natural and easy for us to look at others through a lens of self-righteousness or criticism. Instead we must choose to accept others for who they really are. We must give them the freedom to be themselves in our relationship. If we fail at this, we lose the ability to go deeper in the relationship.

Senior Guide's Dispatch

Camp 3, May 3

C3 is on the Lhotse Face, which is a five-thousand-foot sheet of ice at an average angle of forty-five degrees. C3 is literally cut out of the hard blue ice. This is not an easy place to get around in. To walk around outside, you must wear crampons and be clipped into a fixed line anchored to the mountain. If you fell without being properly roped you may not stop again until you reach C2! We are all being very careful, except for Matt, who doesn't have the patience for all the safety precautions.

We are near the end of our second rotation up here at C3. We have been here for four days after spending a couple days back down at C2. Everyone tells me they feel much stronger now than the first time we climbed to C3. We will spend another day here, then start our descent back down the "hill" to Base Camp, and then several days of R & R in Debouche before starting our summit attempt. Sleeping, eating, and breathing lots of thick air! Our Sherpa team has been busy getting C4 ready, and it should be set tomorrow. We are still on track for a mid-May summit bid. Two teams have already fixed ropes on the South Col route to the summit. Those teams will be making an earlier summit bid than us, but at least the hard work of fixing rope will be done.

Its dinnertime, and I've got to help in the feeding and watering of my crew. Cooking, eating, and cleaning up on the forty-five-degree face of a huge slab of ice is quite an experience. It has been cool the last few days, which has been a blessing since the sun at this altitude can be brutal.

Camp 3, May 4

We are holding here at C3 today as we are being battered by fifty m.p.h. winds. Unfortunately, the weather reports say the winds could get worse before they get better. We are trying to be patient, but all of us want to get back to lower elevations so we can recuperate for our summit push. Matt is struggling the most with being delayed. I told the team that I could not risk climbing down in these conditions, especially the risk of frostbite. But sitting still is hard for Matt. He feels like he is wasting time, and his fear is that time could run out before we have a good shot at the summit. He knows the window of opportunity is small. But I told him this is the way it is on Everest. The biggest game in climbing is the waiting game. This mountain tests everyone differently, and Matt has to learn to slow down, maybe for the first time is his life.

I invited everyone to my tent for beef stroganoff. Ever try to cook in fifty mph winds? Everyone showed but Matt, who said he wasn't feeling well. No one believed him. Jan volunteered that Matt's intensity was wearing thin on the rest of the team. Dan and Rob agreed. I talked with them about the patience and diligence that Everest requires and how hard that was for some people to learn. Many times the best climbers are aggressive personalities like Matt. But they have to learn their limits to have success on Everest. Many of the greatest climbers have died pushing their limits. Everest is the great equalizer and can never be taken for granted.

Since I have been with this group 24-7 for several weeks now, I felt I could dig a little deeper. I told them while I had observed that Matt was not always a friendly, encouraging presence, his tenacity had literally pushed the team forward several times during difficult situations. I reminded the others of the time we were climbing through the Icefalls and the clouds suddenly departed as the sun rose, making it feel like an inferno. His relentless drive to get through the Icefalls to C1 despite those conditions made everyone angry, but also gave them the motivation to make it.

Dan chimed in that he did not feel safe around Matt at times. I told Dan that I had seen Matt take a few chances with his own safety, like moving from tent to tent at C3 without clipping on to the fixed rope, but that I had never seen him do anything that would put anyone else at risk.

Finally, I told them that Matt was just a hard-driving, aggressive person at his core. He would never change because that was how God made him. I understood that his personality style could be irritating, and none of us were immune to it. But we all irritate him too. Dan chuckled and mumbled something about folding his clothes twelve times before putting them

*away. I asked them to try harder to accept Matt for his
strengths and be patient when his strengths were pushed to the
extreme. They agreed to try.*

CAMP 3, MAY 5

*Still too windy to move on the mountain today. Base
Camp tells us the winds should subside by nightfall. I was
late for lunch because I met with our Sherpa team about their
progress at finalizing C4 and getting enough oxygen there for
our summit attempt. When I came in the mess tent, I heard
everyone laughing hysterically. Matt was using our satellite
phone to order a pizza from his favorite place in New York
City. He had them going until he told them that he needed the
delivery to go to C3 on Mount Everest. Since it was just a bit
outside their delivery area, they declined. Everyone had a
good laugh, especially Jan who put him up to it. They all
seemed to be in good spirits, even though we were stuck in
neutral for another day. It seems the gang took my words to
heart and were trying their best to make Matt a part of the
group.*

*The sun had set and the winds have died down, so we
will be up before dawn to start down to Base Camp. We can't
wait for hot showers. And Matt is going to get his pizza. Rob
asked me if the cooks at Base Camp ever made it. It won't be
New York style, but our cook team is willing to give it a try.
I hope Matt likes Asian noodles on his pizza!*

Richard

Moving Higher

Acceptance is the next step after commitment and honesty, but it is not an
easy step to make. It is natural and easy for us to look at others through a
lens of self-righteousness or criticism. Instead we must choose to accept others for who they really are. We must give them the freedom to be themselves
in our relationship. If we fail at this, we lose the ability to go deeper in the
relationship.

OUR PROBLEM WITH GRACE AND MERCY

In even the best of small groups, a time will come when grace and mercy clash with a more legalistic mindset. Victor Hugo's novel *Les Miserables* is a wonderful example of two people, thrown together, who represent the extremes in people, just like the people who will be in your small group. Set in nineteenth-century France, *Les Miserables* tells the story of Jean Valjean, one of "the miserable ones" from the oppressed peasantry. Jean Valjean is a thief whose life is changed by the compassion shown to him by a Catholic priest. Valjean's antagonist throughout the story is police inspector Javert, who makes it his life's mission to capture Valjean and return him to prison. Valjean eludes Javert time and time again. In the last section of the novel, Valjean shows the depth of his compassion by sparing Javert's life when he has the opportunity to take it. This act of compassion shatters Javert's strict moral code, leaving him in anguish. He cannot forgive Valjean for his past crimes, and because of that, he cannot accept Valjean's present act of mercy. For Javert, either justice or mercy can exist but not both. So he ends his life by throwing himself into the river Seine.

Javert is seen as one of the most tragic figures in all of literature, primarily because we so easily see ourselves in him. From everyday mercies like a birthday gift or a meal when you are sick, to the lavish mercy God bestowed on us through Jesus Christ, we struggle with humbly accepting the compassion or kindnesses shown to us. Perhaps the greatest obstacle people have to believing the gospel is the fact that it is the free gift of God.

Now let's move that deep-seated view of law or grace down to how it can affect us in our small groups.

WE WANT TO DO IT THE
OLD FASHIONED WAY—EARN IT

No matter the reason, it is difficult to get past our innate belief that we have to earn everything we get. Whether it is God's free gift of salvation or the undeserved forgiveness of a friend, we feel the need to earn it. It may be freely given, but we have a hard time accepting it as free. After all, we live in a culture where "there is no free lunch" and "you get what you pay for" are two of the most universally accepted maxims.

For many of us, the only way we know that we have God's love is if we keep doing good works to please him. As long as we do things for God, he is in our debt and, in a sense, *owes* us his love. We are resistant to receiving his love under any other conditions. We want to pay for it.

Think about how someone who sees rules as the key to relationships can conflict with someone who sees grace in every relationship. For example, take the apostle Paul. A Pharisee of Pharisees, he absolutely saw having to "earn it" as the basis for relationships. Yet in coming to Christ, he made a huge transition. You can see that movement from having to "do it all myself" to one of trusting God and leaning on his grace in the way Paul asks three times that his "thorn in the flesh" be taken from him. Each time the Lord's answer was, "My grace is sufficient for you, for power is perfected in weakness." And Paul responded with, "Most gladly, therefore, I will rather boast about my weaknesses, so that the power of Christ may dwell in me" (2 Cor. 12:9). Only God's strength is enduring. Only God's power is ultimately reliable. Paul stopped relying on his own strength and his own efforts, and he accepted, acknowledged, and, finally, triumphed through his weaknesses. Paul ended all his attempts to gain God's approval and accepted God's free gift of love and acceptance. Only then was God's power unleashed in his life.

Think about being in a small group where the focus is on law, rules, and measuring up. You can spend week after week feeling like you never measure up. But there is another way—a small group that offers acceptance, grace, and mercy.

JESUS LOVES ME, THIS I KNOW

"Jesus Loves Me" is a hymn used by missionaries all over the world to teach the simple message of the gospel and is widely acclaimed as the most popular hymn of all time. How many times have you heard "Jesus Loves Me"? How many times have you sung it? If you are like many, you can recite its simple, direct message by rote, but perhaps it has lost its meaning. Does Jesus really love us? He knows *everything* about us so how could he? Maybe he only loves us because he has to. His nature is love, so he *has* to love us, doesn't he? He may love us, but does he accept us? Does he accept me even though he knows the truth about me?

Jesus answered that question through an incredible act of humility and love toward his disciples (John 13). Biblical scholars differ on when and where, but some time shortly before the night he was betrayed, he gathered the disciples for a meal, and, during the meal, he got up and washed their feet. At first glance this act may not seem to have great import. But on reflection we can see that it is a profound act with surpassing meaning. Through this act Jesus both demonstrates his profound love for us and models the way we should love, accept, and serve others.

Culturally at this time, we know that only servants of the lowest rank were responsible for washing the dirt off the feet of guests of the homes they served. No one of a higher station in life performed this lowly service. For Jesus, Lord of the universe, to wash anyone's feet was an act of incomprehensible condescension. It is one thing to perform such an act to gain favor with a higher-up, but for Christ to do this for his disciples, the ones who followed and depended on him, was pure humility. The Master serving the servant, even the servant who was about to betray him.

The interplay between Jesus and Peter is particularly instructive. Whether Peter was first, last, or somewhere in between, when Jesus came to him, Peter asked him, "Lord, do You wash my feet?" (v. 6). Peter implies in his question that surely it should be the other way around, with Peter doing the washing. But Peter also questions what Jesus says must happen. Jesus responds by telling Peter that he doesn't understand what he is doing now but he will later.

How often do we question God's ways in the same manner? Jesus knew many things that his disciples didn't know. Just as God knows everything before it happens to us and orders everything that does happen for our benefit (Rom. 8:28). Despite our considerable human limitations, we still deign to question what God does.

But Peter raises the stakes even further. He exclaims, "Never shall You wash my feet!" (v. 8). His words are spoken with finality and an outward appearance of humility, but there is pride beneath them. Peter has gone beyond questioning to refusing what Jesus intends to do. Christ's answer is quick and cutting. He tells Peter, "If I do not wash you, you have no part with Me" (v. 8). Peter immediately sees the error of his ways. His self-will is broken by the thought of a broken realtionship with Jesus. And if not having his feet washed means separation from Christ, then Peter wants to go headlong in the other direction. "Lord, then wash not only my feet, but also my hands and my head" (v. 9). How quickly Peter changed his mind, going from stubborn disobedience to joyful obedience. Would that we could do the same when we are convicted of our own sin.

After Jesus washed their feet, he taught them to serve one another in the same way saying, "For I gave you an example that you also should do as I did to you." He added, "If you know these things, you are blessed if you do them" (vv. 15, 17), a recognition that, even among the disciples who would soon have the power of the Holy Spirit, the doing could fall short of the knowing.

Soon after this display of love and acceptance for his disciples, Jesus demonstrated an even more extreme love by dying for each one of us, purchasing our salvation with his precious blood.

How We Should Act When We're Clean

After Jesus washed Peter's feet, he told Peter he was completely clean (v. 10). By letting Jesus wash his feet, Peter was letting Jesus love him, letting Jesus accept him and declare him clean. Jesus is offering the same thing to each of us. As believers in Jesus Christ, we are clean. We are loved.

And we are accepted. Not perfect. Not sinless. But saved, redeemed, and *acceptable* to our heavenly Father. What should be our response?

When we are transformed by the love and acceptance of Christ, our response will be to love and accept one another just as intensely and just as certainly. Not only will we desire to do it, but we will also have the ability to do it. Your small group will be changed as a result.

Jesus offers the most complete love any of us will ever know. It is unconditional. It does not depend on anything good within us. It is wholly dependent on what is good and pure and holy about the One loving us. When we accept his love, we gain the ability to love others like that. The apostle Paul encouraged us to love and accept all those whom God loves and accepts. "Therefore, accept one another, just as Christ also accepted us to the glory of God" (Rom. 15:7). It is our privilege to be God's instruments for carrying out his work by loving his people. When God's love flows through us to others in our small groups, they see God in us. They feel loved and accepted by us, and they begin to lose the need to prove themselves and the desire to keep the facade around them. People respond to that kind of love, and it draws them closer to God. They see the love of Christ in us, and that makes them want to know him more.

Still this can be a tall order for many in your small group because loving and accepting others unconditionally is hard work. It involves vulnerability, risk, and the possibility of rejection. C. S. Lewis, in his book *The Four Loves*, addressed this by saying: "Love anything and your heart will be wrung and possibly broken. If you want to make sure of keeping it intact you must give it to no one, not even an animal. Wrap it carefully round with hobbies and little luxuries; avoid all entanglements. Lock it up save in the casket or coffin of your selfishness. But in that casket—safe, dark, motionless, airless—it will change. It will not be broken; it will become unbreakable, impenetrable, irredeemable. To love is to be vulnerable."[1] That's why Jesus told the disciples they were "blessed" if they followed his example by loving, accepting, and serving others. He wanted them to know that God was involved in doing the difficult thing he asked them to do, watching and rewarding their efforts.

God is not asking us to do anything that he didn't do first. God has shown his love for us. God has accepted us as we are, with all of our weaknesses and all of our faults. God has freely given us grace and mercy. We should be sharing both of these gifts with others in our small group. Loving acceptance can become a lifestyle choice for your small group, and when it does, your small group will be radically different than it is now. Your small group can be a testimony to the unconditional, transforming love of God.

Note

1. C. S. Lewis, *The Four Loves* (New York: Harcourt, Brace and Company, 1960).

Chapter Seven

Trust—Preparing for the Summit

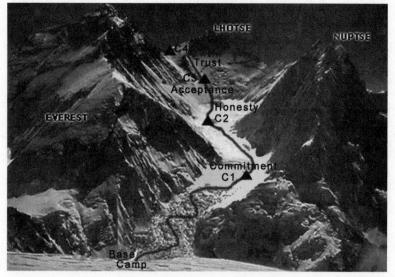

REACHING C4—TRUST

WILLINGNESS AND DESIRE are needed on the part of every member in your small group to be changed by God and to move through the stages of commitment, honesty, and acceptance. Reaching the stage of trust is another mark of spiritual maturity. To do so means becoming a trustworthy person, someone with relational integrity. Without trust a small group can be together for years and never get past a shallow, superficial level. Trust is the safety net that allows your group to brave the heights of authentic relationships.

SENIOR GUIDE'S DISPATCH

CAMP 4, MAY 15

We are about to crawl into our tents and put on our oxygen masks in a futile attempt to get some sleep. C4, at over twenty-six thousand feet, is not an easy place to breathe, let alone eat, drink, or sleep. Even with supplemental oxygen, none of us will get a good night's rest on our first night in the Death Zone. The Death Zone, an altitude of over twenty-six thousand feet, is where most human beings lose their ability to acclimate and their bodies begin to shut down. Not surprising since this altitude is more suited to 747s than people! Each breath pulls in about a third of the oxygen that you get at sea level. Up here your best friend is a full bottle of oxygen!

Tomorrow we will make final preparations and begin our summit push. We have all the oxygen we need, and all the fixed ropes are in good shape. There is still a long way to go, and there is a lot of steep ground before we get to the summit at just over twenty-nine thousand feet. No one can accurately describe how hard it is to drag yourself up that last three thousand feet when it feels like you are breathing through a narrow paper straw. If we make the summit, we will have earned it. This is definitely not for the faint of heart, and my team knows it now if they didn't before.

Just a few days ago we were down in Debouche sleeping in, eating like pigs, and getting a hot shower every day! Now we are just hours away from a summit attempt. We are praying for good weather. Several teams are here waiting for their own summit attempts. I hope we don't have a traffic jam at the Hillary Step, a seventy-foot rock step that only one climber can climb at a time. I am getting conflicting stories about the weather, but the wind is picking up as I speak.

CAMP 4, MAY 16

Just a quick note as we are in a hurry to get going. We are going down not up. We are on our way to C2. High winds

*are making a summit attempt very risky, and I made the call
to go to a lower elevation to wait it out. Other teams are
going ahead with their summit attempt, which makes it hard
on my team to leave. They are confused and a bit angry, wondering why others are allowed to go. I told them we had to
leave now if we wanted to make C2 before dark and that
I would discuss it with them there.*

CAMP 2, MAY 16

*I just left my team in the dining tent. I told them they
needed to decide whether they wanted to attempt a summit
with me or not. I honestly don't know what they will choose.*

*We got down to C2 in record time, probably because of
anger-induced adrenaline. As soon as we stowed our gear, we
met to discuss my decision to move back down to C2 and wait
for the bad weather to clear. What an emotional meeting. I let
them vent for the first twenty minutes, and they let me have
it. No fewer than four teams were attempting to summit as we
met, and several more teams were staying at C4 getting ready
to go. This made my decision look bad. Matt (of course) was
the spokesperson for the group, and in a strong voice (he was
yelling) asked the rationale for my decision to go down rather
than attempt a summit. My team was visibly shocked by my
answer: "Because I've grown to care about you so much."*

*I told them I had seen too many climbers hurt or killed by
the "just do it" mentality that is becoming more prominent on
Everest these days. These people simply can't restrain themselves and show a little patience. We all heed the warnings of
the mountain differently, but high wind and high altitude
don't mix. In my mind there was no reason to risk the lives of
several people I was very fond of. I asked them to trust me.
I told them I would not go back up until I felt we had a realistic chance of making the summit and getting everyone back
safely. I told them Everest would have the last word, but, in my
opinion, none of the groups attempting the summit now would
succeed.*

*Words can't explain how tired I am physically and men-
tally. I know I did the right thing, but will my team trust my
judgment?*

CAMP 2, MAY 17

Even in the slightly thicker air at C2, I didn't sleep well.
I was as worried about the other teams on the mountain as
I was about my team. It didn't take long to find out I had
been right. All of the teams attempting the summit turned
back because of weather. Two of the climbers came back with
frostbite, one with a severe case on his fingers and toes. My
team found out at the same time I did and came to my tent
with sheepish looks to apologize. They all felt bad for not
trusting my judgment, especially when I had never given
them reason to doubt me before. Besides that, they knew
I wanted the summit as badly as they did. Emotions can run
high when you are working on the dream of a lifetime. When
emotion runs high, it can ruin a team. I'm thankful it didn't
happen to mine.

We are off to C4 again in the next hour or so. We will
stay the night and be ready to go early tomorrow morning.
C2 will soon be crowded with the teams that made unsuccessful summit bids. The wind has died down here, but reports say
it is still blowing at the summit. The weather forecasts are
mixed about tomorrow, but I feel a strong inclination to go
back up. I know God is with us, and that gives me strength to
try again.

Richard

Moving Higher

It takes a willingness and desire to be changed by God on the part of every member in your small group to move through the stages of commitment, honesty, and acceptance. Reaching the stage of trust is another mark of spiritual maturity. To do so means becoming a trustworthy person, someone with relational integrity. Without trust, a small group can be together for years and never get past a shallow, superficial level. Trust is the safety net that allows your group to brave the heights of authentic relationships.

WHOM CAN YOU TRUST?

Jim was walking along the edge of a steep cliff one day when he
lost his footing and fell. On the way down, he grabbed a small bush

growing out of the side of the mountain that temporarily stopped his fall. He looked down and, to his horror, saw that the canyon below him fell straight down more than a thousand feet. He couldn't hang onto the branch forever, and there was no way for him to climb back up the steep wall of the cliff.

So Jim began yelling for help, hoping that someone passing by would hear him.

"Help! Help! Is anyone up there? Help!" He yelled for a long time, but no one heard him. He was about to give up when he heard a voice.

"Jim. Jim, can you hear me?"

"Yes, yes! I can hear you. I'm down here!"

"I can see you, Jim. Are you all right?"

"Yes, but who are you, and where are you?"

"I am God, Jim. I'm everywhere."

"You mean *the* God?"

"Yes, that's me."

"God, please help me! I promise if you get me down from here, I'll stop sinning. I'll be a really good person. I'll serve you for the rest of my life."

"Go easy on the promises, Jim. Let me get you out of trouble, then we can talk. Now, here's what I want you to do. Listen carefully."

"I'll do anything, God. Just tell me what to do."

"OK. Let go of the branch."

"What?"

"I said, 'Let go of the branch.' Trust me to save you. Let go."

There was a long silence.

Finally Jim yelled, "Help! Help! Is anyone else up there?"

Sometimes even trusting God is difficult. We have been conditioned most of our lives not to trust others. It is easier for us to trust things than people. We trust the car will start when we turn the key in the ignition. But trusting someone to borrow your car is another thing entirely. When we are young, we are taught never to talk to strangers. We lock our doors at night. We avoid eye contact with people we don't know on the street. We stand apart from other people in line. And don't even think about talking to someone on an elevator!

Healthy relationships foster trust. Trust is the next critical step on the path toward intimacy for your small group. When we live trusting each other, we take the next step in moving from superficial to deeper, more satisfying relationships.

Trust is a sure reliance on the character of another person. When we trust someone, it removes fear from the relationship. When fear is removed, we can share who we really are, confident that the other person will act in our best interests. In the small-group setting, we must not only foster trust but also be diligent in protecting the trust placed in us by others.

THE NEED FOR TRUST

God knows the fullness of eternity past, present, and future and how each of us fits into that picture. Everything he does is for our good and he loves us unconditionally. Still, we struggle to trust him completely. And if we don't see God as worthy of our trust, how can we see one another as trustworthy? Even those we share life with, like those in our small groups.

God blessed each of us with a capacity for trusting others. Some people trust indiscriminately. That is, they trust without having or needing a basis upon which to do so. They simply expect that other people can be relied upon. These people are often called optimists. Others need some proof before relying on someone as trustworthy. They will take a calculated risk by trusting someone and, if it pays off, then they may venture farther out onto the limb. Still others need a substantial amount of evidence before they will trust someone. These people are often called skeptical. We all have the capacity to trust, but trust can be fragile.

We have to be able to rely on others to do what they say they will, and they need to be able to rely on us to do the same. Think of your closest friend, the person you confide in the most. You trust him or her. Why? Probably because you have found them to be trustworthy. But in part it is because you have to. We can go to great lengths to ensure someone keeps his or her word, through verbal or written agreements or the like, but in the end, it all comes down to trust. Without trust, any kind of meaningful relationship with someone else is impossible.

BECOMING TRUSTWORTHY FIRST

Because no one is absolutely trustworthy, our trust is sometimes misplaced. Others let us down. When this happens, trust and relationships based on trust are damaged. Trust is hard to earn and constantly evaluated during a relationship. Trust is easily squandered if we are not careful. As hard as it is to build trust among members in a small group, it is just as easily destroyed by any breach of that trust, intentional or not.

When it comes to trust, we often focus on the trustworthiness of others and just assume our own trustworthiness. But we should become people who are trustworthy first and then look to others in whom we can trust. Trust is not depleted through use; it is built up and multiplies. And being trustworthy breeds trust in others. Instead of *demanding* trust from others, we can *create* trustworthiness in others by first being trustworthy ourselves. A great example of this happening in Scripture involves the apostle Paul (Acts 9).

Imagine being one of the disciples shortly after Christ's death and having Paul come into your midst claiming to have been converted. All you know is that this man participated in the murder of Stephen, zealously persecuted Christians, scattered the church in Jerusalem, and put many of your brothers and sisters in Christ in jail. And now he comes to Jerusalem, claiming that he was miraculously converted and that the Pharisees in Damascus were trying to kill him. If you were fearful that this was an elaborate trap and more than a little skeptical about the truth of Paul's conversion, it would be understandable.

After his arrival, after you heard his conversion story and witnessed him preaching the gospel in the synagogues, and even after the Pharisees in Jerusalem tried to capture and kill him too, it would be understandable if you had lingering doubts about Paul. Paul undoubtedly felt this doubt from some in the church in Jerusalem, but Paul refused to be controlled by his past. He forgot what was behind and focused on what was ahead (Phil. 3:13). He began to be faithful to God's calling on his life. He refused to let the mistrust of others keep him from his mission. In time, because he led a trustworthy life before the disciples, the disciples and Paul soon developed a mutual trust that allowed them to minister effectively together in spite of Paul's past. Rather than demanding trust, Paul created it in those around him. And the same thing can happen in the relationships in your small group.

HOW TO CULTIVATE TRUST

Once your small group has moved through the stages of commitment, honesty, and acceptance, it is ready to move through the stage of trust. Authentic biblical community requires deeper and deeper levels of relating to one another. Cultivating trust within your group requires an active engagement of your heart and soul with the hearts and souls of others. This is not easy. It requires an intentionality and serious effort that is difficult at times. Trusting another person demonstrates a remarkable vulnerability. You are giving someone else the ability to betray that trust and hurt you. But in that process you are also expressing faith in another person, and that faith can help them become trustworthy. Trust breeds trust, and when that happens in your small group, it becomes a safe place where people are free to be real. The fear of being completely known is gone.

The decision to trust someone is typically based on two factors: experience and knowledge. So when someone decides to trust you, it is most likely because he or she has experienced you as trustworthy and knows you well enough to do so. The experience part is pretty straightforward. Do you follow through on your commitments? Are you truthful? Do you make the effort to be clearly understood by others? Do people see others trusting you?

But building trust by experience alone can be risky. Experience may not give someone enough information to build trust in you. Often it takes a deeper understanding of you for the other person to believe placing trust in you is reliable. Do they know your strengths and weaknesses? Do they know how you make decisions? Do others know how you react to stress or pressure? Do you have similar values and goals? This is critical information for others to know about you before they decide to trust you more completely.

However, to get to the point where every person in your small group is known and their true self is revealed can take a significant investment of time. One tool that many small groups are using to dramatically shorten the time it takes to know one another on a deeper level is the Leading From Your Strengths™ assessment. With the help of this assessment, the people in your small group can learn valuable information about themselves and how God wired them. If the people in your group share the basic information in the report with others, information about how and why they do things, how they like and don't like to be communicated with, and how they are adapting to be successful in their current environment, the connection between people needed to cultivate trust will begin to happen almost immediately.

Whether or not they admit it, the members of your small group desperately want this kind of connection. When it happens, members of your small group will be able to trust one another more fully. And your small group will be on the doorstep of intimacy.

Chapter Eight
Intimacy—High Risk and High Reward

★★

THE SUMMIT—INTIMACY

MOST CLIMBERS AGREE that the defining characteristic of a person who reaches the summit of Mount Everest is not talent, experience, or knowledge, but willpower. It takes willpower to reach the summit of intimacy too. You have to be relentless in the pursuit of ever closer, ever deepening relationships in your small group to reach this level. Unconditional love is what sustains you on the summit of intimacy. Without it you cannot survive for long here. The summit of intimacy transforms the people who reach it. Once there they will never settle for lesser heights in their relationships again.

SENIOR GUIDE'S DISPATCH

BASE CAMP, MAY 18, 3:30 A.M.

Hello from Colleen, manager extraordinaire here at Base Camp. I just made radio contact with the team and they have started their summit bid. Richard said the climb is going well so far. It is cold, but the conditions are otherwise excellent. We will pray the good weather holds out until they reach the summit and get back to C4. I have been up all night and will stay up until the team is safely back to C4. I'm too nervous to sleep!

BASE CAMP, MAY 18, 4:50 A.M.

The team is now at The Balcony. The sun is just starting to come up but there won't be full sun for a few hours. I know they will appreciate getting warmed up a bit after a really cold night. Richard tells me Jan is not feeling well. He will monitor her closely as they move on. The next major obstacle is the Hillary Step, another thousand feet up the mountain. This is a seventy-foot steep rock climb with fixed ropes. At sea level this wouldn't be too tough, but at this altitude it may be the most technically challenging part of the climb. The weather is still great with blue skies and few clouds. Keep praying!

BASE CAMP, MAY 18, 9:15 A.M.

I have good news and bad news. The good news is that most of the team has made it through the Hillary Step. They are now only about twenty to thirty minutes from the summit. Unfortunately, Jan and Matt had to turn back. Richard reported that Jan was really not doing well and did not have the strength to make it through the Hillary Step. Richard did not say what Matt's problem was. Congratulations to Jan and Matt for making it that far. They made the right decision to turn back and not risk their lives. It's a difficult decision, but the best philosophy is not to take a chance and live to climb another day.

BASE CAMP, MAY 18, 10:00 A.M.

Hooray, the team has reached the summit! Great job! Congratulations to guide Richard Welch, to team members

Dan Egenolf and Rob Tompson and to Sidar Lakpa Temba Sherpa, Pemba Rita Sherpa, and Tenzing Sherpa for a successful summit. We will be monitoring their descent back to C4. We will all let out a big sigh of relief when they get there!

BASE CAMP, MAY 18, 4:00 P.M.

The team is safely back at C4. They are enjoying some well-deserved rest along with hot tea and soup. Tomorrow they will climb down to C2 for a night before coming back to Base Camp. Even at twenty-one thousand feet, C2 will feel like heaven with its thicker air. The team will eat something and bed down soon. I am going to visit the sandman too since I have been up for about eighteen hours straight. Jan is feeling much better, and Matt is fine. Richard said there was quite a story behind their decision to turn back. I tried to pry it out of him but couldn't. He will be transmitting from C2 tomorrow, so I will find out along with all of you. Thanks for hanging in there with me!

> *Colleen*

CAMP 2, MAY 19

It's great to be able to communicate with you directly again! We are stopping at C2 for the night because the Icefalls have been unstable the last few days, and we want to hit them in the morning when it is cool. We should be back at Base Camp by lunchtime tomorrow. The team is in the dining tent having an amazing meal prepared by our fine cook staff here at C2, so I have some time to fill you in on what happened on the mountain.

First, I have to say that our patience was rewarded with the best weather you could hope for on a summit bid. There was virtually no wind, except for a light breeze that kept us from getting overheated when the sun came out. I know it sounds weird to talk about being overheated while attempting to summit Everest, but it can happen.

On our approach to The Balcony, Jan told me she was not feeling well. She felt weak and developed severe stomach cramps. I checked her oxygen flow, which was fine, and told her to eat some protein gel. We didn't get far past The

Balcony before we had to stop again. Jan's stomach cramps
were getting worse. It was clear she couldn't go on, and
I advised her to turn back, but as always, it is the climber's
decision. She reluctantly and tearfully agreed. I decided to
send two of our Sherpas back to C4 with her. Matt interrupted
and insisted that he would go back with her. To say I was
stunned is putting it mildly. I couldn't believe he would give
up his dream when it was just within his grasp. He was the
most sold out on making the summit the entire trip. I tried to
talk him out of it. I told him the Sherpas were much more
experienced climbers and could get Jan down without his
help. He would hear none of it. If she was going, he was
going. We had to get moving, so I agreed and sent them on
their way. I think I stood there for five full minutes watching
them start their descent, in awe of what had just happened.

When we got back to C4 later that afternoon, Matt came
out to greet us with hot tea. Jan was still weak and was rest-
ing in her tent but was in good spirits. She told us she was
convinced she got food poisoning from something she ate in
Debouche. (The doctor at Base Camp later confirmed her sus-
picions.) I pulled Matt aside and asked him why he quit his
climb to help Jan." He smiled as he replied, "Because I've
grown to care about you all so much." He repeated back to me
the same words I had said to the team two days before. Matt
insisted he would have done the same thing for any of us. He
said it was no big deal. I told him I disagreed. It was a big
deal. It meant that he had grown a great deal as a person on
this climb. It meant that he had developed relationships that
meant something to him, relationships that were worth his
personal sacrifice. I told him he got something more valuable
out of this trip than standing on top of the world.

It's time to go join my team's celebration. I e-mailed my
partners in Mountaintop Expeditions, and they agreed that
I should offer Jan and Matt a return trip to Everest on us. It
should take all of two seconds for them to agree to try again.
I can't wait to climb with them again. One thing is for sure;
we won't be short on laughs or intensity!

BASE CAMP, MAY 21

*Base Camp is becoming a ghost town. There are a couple
more teams on the mountain, but everyone else is gone. We
have the yaks loaded and are heading out on our trip back
down to Lukla, then to Nepal, and then home. Thanks for being
there for us and for all your prayers. This climb was special to
me, more than any other I have been on. My team is leaving
Mount Everest changed. We shared an extremely difficult but
profound experience. Our friendship with one another was
cemented on the mountain. None of us will ever be the same.*

    Richard

Moving Higher

Most climbers agree that the defining characteristic of a person who reaches the summit of Mount Everest is not talent, experience, or knowledge, but willpower. It takes willpower to reach the summit of intimacy too. You have to be relentless in the pursuit of ever closer, ever deepening relationships in your small group to reach this level. Unconditional love sustains you on the summit of intimacy. Without it you cannot survive for long here. The summit of intimacy transforms the people who reach it. Once there they will never settle for lesser heights in their relationships again.

AN EXAMPLE OF LOVE

William Gladstone, a well-known member of parliament and British prime minister, in announcing the death of Princess Alice to the House of Commons in 1878, told the story of how she died. The little daughter of the princess was seriously ill with diphtheria. The doctors told the princess not to kiss her daughter and endanger her life by breathing the child's breath. Once when the child was struggling to breathe, the mother took the little one into her arms to keep her from choking to death. Rasping and struggling for her life, the child begged, "Mummy, kiss me!" Without any thought for herself and in spite of the doctor's warnings, Princess Alice tenderly kissed her daughter. She contracted diphtheria, and soon went to be with her daughter and her Lord.

What is it about this mother's love that strikes a chord deep within us? Her love was selfless. Her love was unconcerned with the consequences of loving. Her love caused her to count the cost and then take action. Yet even this mother's love is but a poor reflection of God's love for us. God showed us how deep his love is by giving his only Son to die for us, even when we were his enemies. Jesus showed us how deep his love is by submitting to his Father's will and offering himself as a sacrifice to atone for our sins. And just before he went to the cross, Jesus commanded the disciples to love one another the same sacrificial way. "A new commandment I give to you, that you love one another, even as I have loved you, that you also love one another" (John 13:34).

Jesus did not give his followers a suggestion or a recommendation but a commandment. And he instructed them to love one another, not as a mother would love her child but as he had loved them. In doing so, Jesus set the stage for intimacy in the lives of the disciples. Christ's example of unconditional love can also be the foundation for intimacy in your small group. His love enables, motivates, and even compels us to love others the way he did.

Having shown them by example how to love one another, he commands them to do likewise. Why was it necessary for him to give them a command? Why would they not follow his example on their own? Because Jesus knew the disciples (and us) too well. He knew the kind of love he was calling them to is opposed to human nature. It goes against human reasoning and logic. Unconditional love like this runs counter to our human sense of fairness and justice. Something in us rebels against this kind of love.

How do we tend to love others? Conditionally. We love others but only to a certain point. We will love them this much but no more. We will love others but only if they prove themselves deserving of our love. This is the kind of love we are comfortable in *giving*.

Contrast this with how Jesus loves us. His love is genuine and honest. He loves us freely, without condition or expectation. It is not based on feelings or emotions. It is willing and sacrificial. There are no limits to his love. This is the kind of love we desire to *receive*. No doubt there is a great cost to loving like this. But the cost of *not* loving like this is higher still.

THE NEED FOR INTIMACY

God created us for intimate fellowship with him. And we are unique in our capacity to fellowship intimately with him and one another. We can *choose* to have meaningful, deep relationships with one another. The greatest longing of our hearts is to be completely known and unconditionally accepted by another person. At the highest level we can fill this longing only through our relationship with God. If our relationship with God is not alive and active or, worse yet, if it doesn't exist at all, we can't hope to find real intimacy with others. But if our relationship with God is healthy and growing, intimate relationships with other people become a critical part of filling that longing in our hearts as well. God created us this way.

Consider the Great Commandment given by Jesus. The Pharisees were trying to best the Sadducees in tripping up Jesus, so they gathered together, and one of them asked Jesus, "Teacher, which is the great commandment in the Law?" (Matt. 22:36). Jesus replied by giving two commandments rooted in the Old Testament Law, the first dealing with man's relationship to God and the second with man's relationship to his fellow man.

He said: "'You shall love the Lord your God with all your heart, and with all your soul, and with all your mind.' This is the great and foremost commandment. The second is like it, 'You shall love your neighbor as yourself.' On these two commandments depend the whole Law and the Prophets" (vv. 37–40).

If you are seeking for purpose in life, purpose for yourself, purpose for your marriage and family, purpose for your church, or purpose for your small group, you don't need to look any further than these words of Jesus. Jesus took hundreds and hundreds of rules and regulations found in the Law and boiled them down into two commandments: love God and love people. The first is paramount because without loving God with all of our hearts we cannot hope to love people the way Jesus commanded us. It would be like trying to start a car without an engine. The second is necessary if we are to be obedient to Christ's command to be his agents for showing his love to others. Love like this is desperately needed in your small group right now.

COUNT THE COST

Fear gripped the heart of a World War I soldier as he saw his lifelong friend fall in battle. They had enlisted together, trained together, and fought side by side throughout the conflict. The entire area was engulfed in heavy enemy crossfire. Any attempt to rescue his friend was suicidal. Yet the soldier asked his sergeant if he could crawl into the no-man's-land between the trenches of the opposing forces and bring back his friend.

"You can go," said the sergeant, "but it won't do any good. Your friend is probably dead, and you'll only get yourself killed."

The sergeant's words didn't stop him; the soldier went anyway.

Miraculously, he managed to reach his friend and carry him back, but he was mortally wounded in the attempt. As they tumbled to the bottom of the trench, the sergeant checked the condition of both men.

"What a waste!" he exclaimed to the soldier. "Your friend is dead, and you're dying. It just wasn't worth it."

"It was worth it, sir," said the dying soldier.

"What do you mean, it was worth it?" responded the sergeant. "Your friend is dead, and we can't do anything to save you."

"Yes, sir," the soldier answered, "but it was worth it. When I got to him, he was still alive. His last words were, 'Thanks, John, I knew you'd come.'"

If we want to build intimacy in our relationships, we need to recognize that it can only be achieved at a cost. We must be willing to give all of ourselves to the cause. Nothing less will do. Intimate relationships are one of the richest treasures in life. But they don't come cheap.

A great many things can hinder the building of intimate relationships. The pace of our lives often makes us too busy to nurture our families or even our existing friendships, let alone make new ones. There are so many distractions, so many things to do and ways to fill our time that we don't focus on people. These things tend to isolate us and keep us from human interaction. Our human nature can be distrustful of people, reluctant to let our guard down and let people inside the walls of our lives.

To get beyond all this takes intense, intentional effort and dogged persistence. Most experienced climbers agree that the most important attribute needed for a person to make the summit of Everest is willpower. The same is true for building intimacy in your small group. It takes a willingness to devote time to others. To spend time and do life together. It takes a willingness to sacrifice. To give not only of your time but also of your resources and talents. It takes a willingness to be selfless. To ignore your own needs and focus on the needs of others. To give of yourself gladly for them. If need be, to put it all on the line for your friend. It takes a willingness to endure all things. To be steadfast. Through good times and tough times. Intimate relationships are not fickle or fair weather. They are lasting.

A DESTINATION WORTH THE JOURNEY

This is a tall order, to be sure. But wonderful blessings will come from building intimate relationships in your small group. Here are three of the most important.

First, you will be meeting one of the greatest needs of each person in your group. Whether they admit it or not, people are starving for deep, committed relationships. Again, these relationships won't exist between every person in your small group. The goal of building intimacy in your small group is not that every member will have an intimate relationship with every other member. Even Jesus was closer to some people than others. He was close to the disciples as a group and closer still to Peter, James, and John. And John was called "the disciple whom Jesus loved." The goal is to create an atmosphere in your small group where intimate relationships are formed easily and are highly valued and nurtured.

Second, there is a uniquely personal benefit to building intimate relationships with others. Our lives are filled with superficial relationships. Many of these are practical rather than personal. You have relationships with your doctor, dentist, plumber, bank teller, and employer, but they are not necessarily personal. You relate to them professionally not personally. Other superficial relationships exist with people you know from church, sports teams, or school groups, and you may share a few personal things with them, but it usually doesn't go much deeper than asking how things are going and quickly moving on. They may be people you would like to get to know better, but there isn't time.

Intimate relationships are different. You must invest the time to develop them. They must go to a deeper level and reach the personal areas of your life. And intimate relationships must be supportive. This is where unconditional love comes in. In an intimate relationship you should be on the receiving end of the support that comes from a relationship built on love. The other person will help and strengthen you, help bear your burdens. It is not selfish to see this as the great blessing of an intimate relationship. Especially because you should be doing the same for the other person. The relationship will thrive when you try to outdo each other in being supportive rather than being supported.

The most important benefit of intimate relationships is that they build our faith. God designed us for intimacy with other people so that through those relationships we could help one another live by faith in him. A small group that is focused on building intimate relationships is also helping people stay faithful in their walk with God. If no one in your small group is going through a crisis of faith right now, it is virtually certain they will be before too long. When it happens, will they stay true to God and his Word or will their faith crumble? The answer has a lot to do with whether they have intimate relationships in the group. Is there someone with enough relational equity with that person to walk with through the trial and help him or her stay faithful? Intimate relationships can have a profound effect on helping others persevere in the faith. The end result is a small group filled with people trusting God and helping others do the same.

Intimacy is the pinnacle of human relationships. Building intimacy, like anything else worth having, is hard work. It will cost you something. But the cost of not building intimate relationships is greater. Invest what it takes to build intimate relationships, and you will be investing for eternity. These relationships will literally last forever.

Chapter Nine

Build the Small Group You've Always Wanted

JUST LIKE FAMILY

WE ALL WANT the real relationships that can develop in a small group. And we need them. Intimate relationships are one of the best answers to the pervasive feeling of meaninglessness and worthlessness so prevalent today. One way that we can show the unconditional love of Christ to the world is by building intimate relationships in our small groups. These kinds of relationships should flourish among Christians, especially among those involved in small groups. The deeper the relationships, the more the church begins to look like family.

A family that is close-knit and shows unconditional love for one another is irresistible. Everyone knows such a family is not perfect, but the obvious flaws don't seem to matter. People are captivated by the relationships in that family because they are characterized by a genuine loving concern as they talk and walk through life together. The same thing can happen in a small group that cultivates intimate relationships. They become like a family, and they become irresistible to others.

Most successful parents will tell you that being a family is more than being bound by blood. A real family is a place of refuge where family members are loved and accepted absolutely, without demanding performance or perfection. This is the same way that Christ loves us. People can't help but respond to that kind of love. Our prayer is that your small group becomes characterized by this kind of love.

GOING THROUGH THE STAGES

Anyone who attempts to climb Mount Everest quickly learns one valuable lesson: You are not in control; the mountain is. Some climbers take incredible risks doing things like establishing speed records or helping in a rescue and live to tell about it. Other climbers take one small step in the wrong direction and perish. One climber will make the summit, and within minutes the weather will change, and another climber is forced to turn back just a few hundred feet below the summit. The whims of the mountain are hard to understand, but for most experienced mountaineers, it is not reaching the summit that signifies a successful climb. It is the journey that matters most. The process of training, traveling, meeting new people, and testing the strength of mind, body, and spirit is a reward in itself.

That same philosophy is true of building intimacy in small groups. Relationships in your small group will go through the stages of commitment, honesty, acceptance, and trust on the way to intimacy. No matter what you call these stages or what order you put them in, these characteristics must exist for relationships to reach an intimate level. Some of the relationships in your group will only make it through one or more of the stages. Each stage is a worthy goal in itself. On Everest there is a lot of movement between camps. A team will spend several nights higher up on the mountain to acclimate and then come back to Base Camp to recover. The next time that team goes higher, it is easier. Likewise, each stage on the path to intimacy takes time, energy, and effort. And you may not make it to intimacy in any given relationship.

Sometimes relationships just fizzle out. Sometimes people hurt each other. Sometimes people simply move. Whatever the reason, don't be discouraged if some relationships don't get to intimacy. Remember that the next time you try with another relationship, it will be easier. You have been there before. You can guide others through the stages you've already been through. Make an effort to get as far as you can go in your relationships and, if they end, take as much as you can away from the experience.

One final thought on building intimate relationships with others in your small group. Christians are experts at faking it. You can fake a lot of things, like whether you're a Christian, whether you have a growing relationship with Christ, or whether your marriage is struggling. But you can't fake an intimate relationship that is built on love. It's simply impossible to do.

In the end, whether we have developed intimate, loving relationships shows who we really are and whose we really are. Why did Jesus command the disciples to love one another in John 13:34? He tells us in the next verse. "By this all men will know that you are My disciples, if you have love for one another" (John 13:35).

Christ is always here with us. Our job is to make him visible to people who don't know him. Building intimate relationships in your small group will make Christ visible to those around you. At the same time it will transform relationships in your small group. Accomplishing that will give everyone in your small group an amazing feeling. Like you are standing on top of the world!

Part III
Moving Higher

A Four-Week Study on Building Intimacy in Your Small Group

THERE IS ONE SURE WAY to make the most of your small group's journey to intimacy. We have developed a four-week small-group study based on the principles you have learned in this book (Commitment, Honesty, Acceptance, and Trust) and linked it with an amazing relationship-building tool that will not only help you understand your own God-given strengths but will help you understand the strengths of every other person in your group. The Leading From Your Strengths™ assessment takes less than ten minutes to complete, but the results you get can take the relationships in your group to a deeper level faster than you ever thought possible.

We encourage you to stop reading and take the Leading From Your Strengths™ assessment right now. And you can do it for **Free**! We have included a passcode on the inside back jacket of this book that entitles you to take the free assessment. Once you have found the passcode, go to www.leadingfromyourstrengths.com and enter the passcode in the box underneath Small Group Passcode on the home page. Follow the on-screen instructions to take the assessment.

Once you have experienced this powerful assessment tool for yourself, encourage the other members in your group to go to our Web site and purchase a Leading From Your Strengths™ assessment for themselves. Their investment of time and money will pay huge dividends in strengthening the relationships in your small group! We strongly encourage you to have everyone in your small group take the assessment now, before you move on to the four-week small-group study that follows.

The Leading From Your Strengths™ assessment and the other Leading From Your Strengths™ products and materials are based on three core principles:

1. **Understanding Your Own God-Given Strengths**—This is the starting point for personal growth and is essential for developing strong, deep relationships with others.

2. **Understanding and Valuing the Strengths of Others**—Recognizing and respecting the strengths of others is necessary to appreciate the unique relationship dynamics of any group or team.

3. **Blending Differences to Build Unity**—Differences between people can be a stumbling block or, if they are blended together, can promote unity and closeness in relationships

The people who are the most effective at building close-knit relationships are those who understand how God created them and know the unique gifts and strengths they possess. The Leading From Your Strengths™ assessment gives you this knowledge.

In the same way, the assessment gives you valuable information about others in your group. Have you ever wondered why there is tension or even open conflict between you and another person? The cause is most likely to be a difference in your behavioral styles. Unless you know what these differences are, there is no way to resolve conflict if it exists or prevent it from occurring in the first place. But if each person in your small group takes the assessment and shares the results with the group, the source of existing or potential conflict is revealed and relationships have a chance to be healed or strengthened. But the assessment doesn't do it all. Once you and the others in your small group know the unique strengths that make up the group, it is up to each one of you to put that knowledge to work in building stronger relationships. This is the Leading From Your Strengths™ process and it starts with you!

Without understanding the unique strengths of each person in your small group, building intimate relationships is difficult if not impossible. The great advantage of using a tool like the Leading From Your Strengths™ assessment is that you can dramatically shorten the time it takes to get this understanding. By investing just ten minutes to take the assessment, you can learn things about the others in your group that could otherwise take months or years of time together to learn. The Leading From Your Strengths™ assessment helps you do it in a fun, informative and memorable way by using Dr. John Trent's four animal characters: Lion, Otter, Golden Retriever, and Beaver. And the assessment is just the beginning. The Leading From Your Strengths™ process includes a DVD presentation by Dr. Trent and Rodney Cox designed exclusively for small groups that will take your group through a more detailed examination of the principles in this book. You can find all of the Leading From Your Strengths™ materials for small groups at www.leadingfromyourstrengths.com.

Although it is written primarily for small group leaders, the Small Group Study that follows was designed so that *anyone* can facilitate the study and move their small group towards greater intimacy. If you are just starting a small group, the study gives you great tips on starting your small group on the right path. If you are a small group veteran, some of the tips may seem basic, but you should review them to ensure you are getting the most from your small group experience. In any case, the detailed exercises that are part of the study will improve communication and deepen understanding within your group.

Remember, we would love your feedback on this study and to hear your success stories of moving higher toward the summit of intimacy in your small group. Please send us an e-mail at feedback@leadingfromyourstrengths.com.

LEADERS' GUIDE

INTRODUCTION

PREPARATION FOR YOUR FIRST GROUP MEETING

1. As the leader, take the Leading From Your Strengths™ assessment and become familiar with your own report. Encourage the members in your small group to take the assessment as well and bring the report with them. It

will increase people's understanding of themselves and it will cause momentum in the group toward the goal of intimacy.

2. Personal contact is a great way to remind the participants of the meetings. A personal phone call or quick note will show your interest in them.

3. Pray for each person by name in your small group. Pray that each person will grow in knowledge and understanding of themselves, understanding and valuing of others, and learning how to blend any differences.

4. Cover the details, i.e. map or directions to the small group location, babysitting logistics, contact phone number or e-mail for questions, parking, refreshments, where to get the study guide, etc.

5. Make sure teaching tools are available and tested before small group begins, e.g.—Leading From Your Strengths™ DVD, DVD player, dry erase board or large flip chart, and appropriate markers.

6. Make sure each person has a copy of this study guide. Prepare for the lesson yourself and encourage others to do the same.

LEADING YOUR SMALL GROUP

1. Start on time. If you start promptly, people in your group will realize the importance of being on time.

2. Open in prayer. Ask God to speak through the Bible and the study as the group grows toward intimacy.

3. Encourage participation by each person. Some will be more verbal than others. Ask "how" and "why" questions rather than "what" or "who" questions.

4. Explain that the format is a discussion rather than a tolecture.

5. Don't let one or two people dominate the conversation. This includes you, the leader. Don't answer all of your own questions.

6. Be careful of going on tangents apart from the topic of the evening. You may want to ask, "What do the rest of you think?" to help steer the conversation back on track.

7. Grow in confidence. Learn to be comfortable with silence as some people need time to process information before they respond.

8. End on time. Encourage the people in your group to complete their lesson for next time. In some groups people may want to commit to praying for each other or to calling each other during the week.

WEEKLY "CHAT" FORMAT

As you develop intimacy, one of the major elements will be communication —openly sharing what is on your heart. Therefore, this study guide includes an acrostic "CHAT" to remind you of the importance of talking about "Commitment," "Honesty," "Acceptance," and "Trust," which are the steps to intimacy within your small group. Each week your study guide will develop one of these four "CHAT" steps. The other three steps will be woven throughout.

EACH WEEKLY LESSON IS DIVIDED INTO FIVE PARTS WITH A SUGGESTED ONE-HOUR TIME LIMIT

1. Starting Out (15 minutes)—Welcome, opening prayer, setting the stage for each week's topic. This is a good time to use the Leading From Your Strengths™ DVD.

2. On the Journey (5 minutes)—Thought-provoking questions pertaining to one of the "CHAT" topics.

3. Climbing Higher (15 minutes)—Bible study on the relationships between David, Jonathan, and Saul that demonstrates the challenge of appreciating differences.

4. Team Time (15 minutes)—Case studies about how to understand strengths and blend differences within your small group.

5. View from the Top (10 minutes)—Summary Questions, Looking Forward, and Closing Prayer.

TEAM TIME: UNDERSTANDING STRENGTHS AND BLENDING DIFFERENCES WITHIN YOUR SMALL GROUP

In every small group, there are different types of behavioral styles. Without a clear understanding of this, conflict can develop because you don't see other people's point of view. You are inclined to believe that your way of thinking, acting, and speaking is the right way.

Intimacy within a small group can be difficult to develop if each person is trying to project what they perceive to be their "good self" in order to be accepted by others. People often fear "opening up" in small groups. Perhaps, in the past, you have been disappointed by the response you have (or have not) received from others when you exposed your "true self".

During the Team Time sections of this study guide, we will refer to different characters who typify behaviors that will represent those personalities that also appear in your small group.

You will be asked to respond to a series of questions regarding how the following individuals react with each other in their fictional small group.

Note: The names of these characters are Larry, Olivia, Gary, and Betty. They correspond to the four animal characters in the Leading From Your Strengths™ report: Lion, Otter, Golden Retriever, and Beaver.

Larry is a strong, assertive, take-charge type of person. He is decisive and can be impatient with obstacles in his way. He likes to problem solve and keep moving toward a goal. Larry's biggest fear is losing and wasting his time.

Olivia is fun loving and extremely verbal. She loves groups, parties, and activities. She enjoys change and is very spontaneous and creative but is not detail-oriented. She can see and communicate the "big picture". Olivia's biggest fear is the loss of approval of others.

Gary is a great team player. He is steady and wants everyone to feel close and connected. He is very understanding and compassionate and has difficulty saying "no". He can be soft on people and generally prefers a slower pace and thoughtful decisions. Gary's biggest fear is change and the resulting loss of connection with the familiar.

Betty is a critical thinker and detail oriented. She likes to follow the rules and wants everyone else to do the same. She has high standards for herself and others. She is comfortable in a systematic way of doing things with a slower, steady pace that produces long-term solutions and results. Betty's biggest fear is making a mistake or losing quality in her decisions and actions.

Week #1 of "CHAT"—Building Intimacy through Commitment

Starting Out: 15 minutes

Welcome and Open in Prayer
- Optional: Have everyone turn to the General Characteristics section of the Leading From Your Strengths™ report and allow several people to share two or three statements that they believe are most true of them. As a result of each person sharing these "core" strengths about themselves, the small group can gain increased understanding and appreciation for each group member.
- Optional: Dr. John Trent and Rodney Cox on DVD setting the stage for commitment.

On the Journey: Thought-Provoking Questions about Commitment: 5 minutes
- *Websters's* definition of commitment: A pledge to do something or the state of being bound emotionally or intellectually to a course of action or to another person or persons
- What is your definition of commitment?
- Why is it difficult to commit to other people? (i.e., Negative past experiences regarding honesty, acceptance, trust, time pressure, fear of failure, rejection, etc.)

- What are the parameters or limits of your commitment? (Will you commit to everyone in the small group or just a few individuals of your choice? Are you committing to your small group just while you are in the study or also during the week? After the group ends?)
- Ground Rules: It's important for small groups to establish ground rules. Gather everyone's input and then help the group select approximately five or six that are the most important to everyone as a group. These guidelines will help to develop commitment within the small group.

Examples of Potential Ground Rules
- Attend each week unless there's an emergency.
- Call if not coming or if you will be late.
- Start and end on time.
- Declare "No put-downs."
- Agree that "What is said here, stays here".
- Give others the opportunity to share. (Don't monopolize the conversation.)
- Complete assignments.
- Take the Leading From Your Strengths™ assessment.
- Value each member's uniqueness and differences.

CLIMBING HIGHER: BIBLE STUDY ON THE COMMITMENT BETWEEN DAVID, JONATHAN, AND SAUL: 15 MINUTES

Please read the Scripture passages in paranthesis and then answer the related questions. The story of David and Jonathan demonstrates one of the strongest relationships recorded in the Bible. Please read the biblical accounts and answer the questions below as to the commitments that they made to each other. (Keep in mind that Jonathan was the king's son, but David would be the next king of Israel.)
- What accomplishments or common ground did Jonathan and David have? (1 Sam. 14:6–15, 17:32–50)
- What was it about David's character that attracted Jonathan to him?

Jonathan and David made a covenant to each other.
- What was the motive and what did the gifts represent? How was this a sacrifice on the part of Jonathan? (1 Sam. 18:1–4)
- What types of character traits attract you to other types of people?
- What are you looking for in someone with whom you can be open?

TEAM TIME: CASE STUDY AND APPLICATION QUESTIONS: 15 MINUTES

This time will help you better understand your own unique, God-given strengths as well as how to blend and appreciate differences within your small group.

Case Study on Commitment

During week one, each member of a small group had agreed to specific ground rules. On week two, Olivia arrives to the small group meeting fifteen minutes late and has not completed the agreed upon assignment. She apologizes for being late and gives an excuse that she had a crazy week. She didn't have time to do the assignment, received a phone call she had to take as she was leaving the house, and got stuck in traffic. The following demonstrates how each of the characters might react to Olivia's excuses.

Larry points out that she has violated two of the small group commitments.

Olivia has decided that the standard set for the small group ground rules is too high and asks to change some of the guidelines.

Gary sits silently processing, uncomfortable with the "conflict," and finally says something to keep the peace.

Betty tells Olivia, "You made commitments the first week and there are no second chances; rules are rules".

- Discuss your reactions to the way each of these characters responded to the situation. What are the pros and cons of each position?
- Within your small group, identify any commitments that you have difficulty keeping and discuss the reasons why.
- How should your group handle a breach of commitment?

VIEW FROM THE TOP: SUMMARY QUESTION, LOOKING FORWARD,
AND CLOSING PRAYER: 5 MINUTES

Summary Question
> 1. What are the specific commitments you have or will agree
>   to make as a group? (Refer to the "Ground Rules" section
>   earlier in this lesson if needed.)

Looking Forward
- C: Commitments made on Week #1 (List them and review.)
- H: Honesty: In Week #2, the emphasis will be on honesty. In preparation for that meeting, observe how often you choose to wear a mask in daily life.
- A: Acceptance
- T: Trust

Close in Prayer

Week #2 of "Chat"—Building Intimacy through Honesty

Starting Out: 15 minutes

Welcome and Open in Prayer
- Optional: Have everyone turn to the Style Analysis Graphs page of the Leading From Your Strengths™ report, which has the "Core" Style and "Adapted" Style graphs. Remember that the "Core" Style Graph shows who you really are and the "Adapted" Style Graph shows who you think you need to be in order to be successful in your current environment. People often become someone different than who they really are in order to be successful in a variety of environments. However, if you are constantly adapting, it can cause stress. Discuss how these graphs are similar or different for each person in your small group and what they may mean for them.
- Optional: Dr. John Trent and Rodney Cox on DVD setting the stage for honesty.

On the Journey: Thought-Provoking Questions about Honesty
- *Websters's* definition of honesty: Characterized by integrity or fairness and straight-forwardness in conduct, thought, speech, etc. and not deceptive or fraudulent; genuine

- What is your definition of honesty? (Note: This type of honesty involves being open about who you really are.)
- When are you tempted to be dishonest in your relationships? (That is, do you use a mask to cover-up or be how you think others want you to be?)
- Give an example of a person you know who is transparent and reveals who he or she really is.
- What are the parameters or limits of removing your mask? (Will you be real to everyone in the small group or just a few individuals of your choice?)

CLIMBING HIGHER: BIBLE STUDY ON THE HONESTY ISSUES BETWEEN DAVID, JONATHAN, AND SAUL: 15 MINUTES

Please read the Scripture passages in paranthesis and then answer the related questions. David gains tremendous recognition and respect from the leaders and people with his God-given victory over the giant Goliath. King Saul becomes extremely jealous and does not show his honest feelings to David. Jonathan continues to defend and commit to David.

King Saul seems very pleased with David's courage and rewards him with a high rank in the army. However, within days Saul is very angry, suspicious, and jealous of David when the people praise David more than Saul. (1 Sam. 18:5-16)

- Part of Saul's fear was related to the influence of an evil spirit, but what was the impact of Saul hiding behind his "mask" when he dealt with David?

Jonathan brought a measure of peace between his father, King Saul, and his best friend by giving an honest, positive report about David. (1 Sam. 19:1–10)

- What do you think was the impact of that action on the relationship between David and Jonathan?
- Have you ever had a friend defend you before someone else? As a result, how did the respect and trust grow between you and your friend?
- Honesty is risky and will cost you in your relationships. What are the costs of keeping your mask on and not being honest versus the costs of taking your mask off and being honest but opening yourself up to being hurt?

Team Time: Case Study and Application Questions: 15 minutes

This time will help you better understand your own unique, God-given strengths as well as how to blend and appreciate differences within your small group.

Case Study on Honesty

Jack is hesitant to come to a small group on intimacy because in the last small group he attended, after sharing a personal story of marital infidelity, he felt embarrassed and judged by the others. In his mind, he's thinking, *Why should I remove a mask and be honest when I'm not sure I can trust that these people will accept me?* Observe each of the reactions as the characters respond to Jack's dilemma.

Larry says, "Get over it, give it to God, and move on."

Olivia says, "I'm sure God will use this in the future to help others in a similar situation."

Gary encourages Jack by saying, "That was a different group; we're not like that."

Betty asks detailed questions for clarification to determine why the judgment and embarrassment occurred.

- If Jack were this honest in your group, how would you respond?
- If your group really plans to be intimate, what commitments will you make regarding honesty? (That is, are you honest with everyone or just with one or two people apart from the group?)
- Is it realistic to be honest with everyone in the small group?

View from the Top: Summary Questions, Looking Forward, and Closing Prayer

Summary Questions

1. There can be a wonderful sense of freedom and release from stress when people are honest and transparent in a healthy environment. How have you seen this to be true in your life?
2. What safeguards will you place in your life to maintain your honesty and transparency? Whom will you allow to ask you the tough questions on key areas of your life?

Looking Forward
- **C**: Commitments made on Week #1 (List them and review.)
- **H**: Honesty: In Week #2, the emphasis was on honesty. Continue to consciously remove any masks and be the unique person that God created you to be!
- **A**: Acceptance: In Week #3, the emphasis will be on acceptance. In preparation for that meeting, observe how often you feel accepted by others for who you really are. Even better, how often do *you* accept others?
- **T**: Trust

Close in Prayer

Week #3 of "Chat"—Building Intimacy through Acceptance

Starting Out: 15 minutes

Welcome and Open in Prayer
- Optional: Have everyone turn to the last page of their Leading From Your Strengths™ report, which contains the Ministry Insights Wheel. In the last two session you have looked at each individual's "Core" and "Adapted" styles. During this session focus on your group as a whole. Discuss where each person's "Core" style (the circle) is on the Wheel. This will give you a picture of your entire small group and how the Lord has placed each of you together in a unique way.
- Optional: Dr. John Trent and Rodney Cox on DVD setting the stage for acceptance.

On the Journey: Thought-Provoking Questions about Acceptance: 15 minutes
- *Websters's* definition of acceptance: To receive something offered, especially with gladness or approval; a disposition to tolerate or accept people or situations; or the act of taking something that is offered
- What is your definition of acceptance of other people? (i.e., nonjudgmental reactions)
- After the mask is off, how difficult is it to accept people who are different than you thought them to be?
- List reasons why people do not accept others in small group situations. (For example, members see tendencies they don't like in themselves.)

*CLIMBING HIGHER: BIBLE STUDY ON ACCEPTANCE ISSUES
BETWEEN DAVID, JONATHAN, AND SAUL*

Please read the Scripture passages in paranthesis and then answer the related questions. The growth in the relationship between David and Jonathan is contrasted with the deterioration in the relationship between Saul and David. Jonathan accepted David as he was, while Saul did not.

Jonathan asked David to show kindness to his family forever. Then both David and Jonathan reaffirmed their commitments to each other in the context of deep friendship. (1 Sam. 20:14–17)

- If love and acceptance are not at the core of commitments, what usually happens to those commitments?
- What did Jonathan finally come to accept about his father and about his relationship to David? Because Jonathan was so accepting of who David was, what is the impact on the relationship between Saul and Jonathan? (1 Sam. 20:27–34)
- Sometimes believing in others will cost you. Has this happened to you? If so, explain.

While Saul was seeking to destroy David, Jonathan went to strengthen David. It is interesting to note that after this wonderful exchange between friends they would never see each other again. What wonderful memories. (1 Sam. 23:14–18)

- How does Jonathan show acceptance of who David is now and what he will become in the future?
- Who are several people who really accept you at your core, including family, friends, or individuals from your small group?
- What could you specifically say or do to each person in your group to show your acceptance of them and to bless their lives?

*TEAM TIME: CASE STUDY AND APPLICATION QUESTIONS:
15 MINUTES*

This will help you better understand your own unique, God-given strengths as well as how to blend and appreciate differences within your small group.

Case Study on Acceptance

In week three, Robert, a regular but silent attendee, was ready to take off his mask. He felt comfortable sharing with his small group that he was struggling with alcohol since he recently lost his job, and was frequenting bars looking for friendship. He was embarrassed to tell his other church friends about his situation. However, he thought that his small group might accept him with this information; so he was willing to take the risk. This is how each of the characters reacted to Robert's dilemma. In your opinion, does each person show acceptance in a non-judgmental way?

Larry told Robert to contact a Christian twelve-step program.

Olivia tried to persuade Jeff to come bowling with her and the single's group at church.

Gary told Robert that he would be his friend through this and would go with him to a Christian twelve-step program.

Betty told Robert about several job openings in her company.

- Describe and discuss similar situations in which you have or have not felt acceptance within a small group.
- How often do you observe judgmental attitudes rather than acceptance from Christian brothers and sisters?
- What about you? Would you consider yourself judgmental or accepting of the behavior of others? What is the balance between the two?

VIEW FROM THE TOP: *SUMMARY QUESTIONS, LOOKING FORWARD, AND CLOSING PRAYER*

Summary Question

1. How does "accept one another, just as Christ also accepted you" (Rom. 15:7) impact a potentially critical or judgmental nature?

Looking Forward

- **C:** Commitments made on Week #1 (List them and review.)
- **H:** Honesty: In Week #2, the emphasis was on honesty. Continue to consciously remove any masks and be the unique person that God created you to be.

- A: Acceptance: In Week #3, the emphasis was on acceptance. How are you progressing in your quest to accept behavioral differences in others?
- T: Trust: Week #4 will be your final meeting and the emphasis will be on trust. In preparation for that meeting, prayerfully consider whether or not you have grown in intimacy within your small group.

Close in Prayer

Week #4 of "Chat"—Building Intimacy through Trust

Starting Out: *15 minutes*

Welcome and Open in Prayer
- Optional: The goal of these four weeks has consisted of more than simply observing behavioral tendencies. The deeper goal was to affect positive and lasting change as each person gained a better understanding of his or her own unique, God-given strengths as well as how to blend and appreciate differences within the small group.
- In this final small-group meeting, based on the Leading From Your Strengths™ report, have each person share at least one insight that they have gained, about themselves or the group, that will make a difference to them in the future.
- Optional: Dr. John Trent and Rodney Cox on DVD setting the stage for trust.

On the Journey: *Thought-Provoking Questions about Trust: 15 minutes*

- *Websters's* definition of trust: Firm reliance on the integrity, ability, or character of a person or thing; or something committed into the care of another; charge
- When you divulge who you really are and put personal information into the care of others, you trust that they will have integrity in what they choose to tell others. Why is it often difficult to trust in this way?

- What type of environment is required to foster that trust?

CLIMBING HIGHER: BIBLE STUDY ON TRUST ISSUES BETWEEN DAVID, JONATHAN, AND SAUL

Please read the Scripture passages in paranthesis and then answer the related questions. For a number of years, Saul and his army would chase David in the desert trying to destroy David and his men. Several times David spared Saul's life. King Saul pursued and tried to eliminate David because he did not trust him. To Saul, David was a threat, disloyal, and subversive. Though this was untrue, it seemed to be reality to Saul. (1 Sam. 24:1–3)

- How did Saul spend his life due to perceived mistrust? For David, Saul was not to be trusted. By his behavior and his words Saul had reinforced over time his untrustworthiness. (1 Sam. 24:4–22)
- How did David's commitment to a sovereign and trustworthy God, allow him to be so gracious to King Saul?

When David became king, he remained a trustworthy friend, even though Jonathan had passed away. (2 Sam. 9:1–3, 6–11)

- What did King David do out of respect for Jonathan and the commitments they had made to each other?
- You cannot demand that people trust you. Trust is earned over time by repeatedly being loyal in word, deeds, and attitudes. Considering your close friends or someone in your small group, what are you doing to build trust in those relationships?

TEAM TIME: CASE STUDY AND APPLICATION QUESTIONS: 15 MINUTES

These will help you better understand your own unique, God-given strengths as well as how to blend and appreciate differences within your small group.

Case Study on Trust

It was the last week and Jane was reflective regarding her small group experience. In her opinion, this had been the best small group she had ever attended. During these four weeks, Jane had learned about God, herself, and others as well as how to appreciate the differences in those relationships.

Jane had a track record of quitting small groups half way through because she usually found fault with most of the participants. As she reflected on previous small-group experiences, she was fearful to get involved in a new study because she was not sure any other group could develop this level of intimacy.

Actually, she initially contemplated quitting this study as well but felt she couldn't after the first week on commitment! So she stuck it out.

It wasn't always easy for her to understand where some people were coming from, but she soon learned to value each individual for their uniqueness. Jane struggled with all of the CHAT areas. She found it difficult to stick with the commitment of removing her own mask and also of being honest and accepting. However, now after four weeks of being together in such a wonderful small group, she was amazed and actually overcome with emotion as she reflected on how much she valued each person in the group. Here is a glimpse into her journal that she wrote prior to attending the last small group study:

Larry: "I did not really care for Larry during the first session because of his bluntness. He always seemed impatient if things didn't move fast enough. However, now I admire his directness and honesty. He is very confident in who he is and doesn't change for anyone. He risked giving straight answers and wasn't afraid to hold us accountable to our agreed upon commitments even when he knew we might not like the accountability."

Olivia: "She initially drove me crazy with her giggling and talking. Even though she began keeping her commitment to be on time, she always made a dramatic entry with ten reasons why it was difficult for her to come at all. However, as I observed her more, I realized that she did have a full life. It was full of laughter and joy that she shared with others. She even made Larry laugh. She could always see the big picture and viewed life as something to be enjoyed."

Gary: "He was the most difficult person in the group to figure out because he rarely showed his feelings. He didn't volunteer information about himself, and I was always guessing as to whether or not he even liked me. Then I discovered he was a very good listener because, when he finally did speak, it was obvious that he had thought through his responses and was very empathetic. He faithfully sent personalized and encouraging e-mails to everyone in the small group every week."

Betty: "I was usually exhausted being around her because of her constant attention to detail and insistence on following the rules without exception. She was hesitant to write anything in her study guide until she was sure it was the perfect answer. Then she surprised me with the most beautiful and intricate hand-made quilted wall hanging that she had designed herself. The attention to detail was magnificent. Also, looking back, I do not think we would have stayed focused if Betty wasn't a part of our group, encouraging us to start on time and complete all the assignments."

VIEW FROM THE TOP: SUMMARY QUESTIONS, LOOKING FORWARD, AND CLOSING PRAYER: *10 MINUTES*

Summary Questions:
1. What have you learned about the rewards of trusting others?
2. How have you become a more trusting or trustworthy person?
3. How have you learned to understand yourself and others and then blend the differences?

Looking Forward
- **C:** Commitments made on Week #1 (List them and review.)
- **H:** Honesty: In Week #2, the emphasis was on honesty. Continue to consciously remove any masks and be the unique person that God created you to be.
- **A:** Acceptance: In Week #3, the emphasis was on acceptance. How are you progressing in your acceptance of the differences in others?
- **T:** Trust: Can you declare victory in the area of trust within your small group?

This week concludes the Small Group Study. Genuinely thank everyone for his or her participation in this study.

New Commitment: Where does your group go from here? Are you willing to commit to another small group study together? Don't quit now; there are still mountains to climb on your ascent to intimacy.

Close in Prayer